THIS IS NOT A WRITING MANUAL

Notes for the Young Writer in the Real World

KERRI MAJORS

WRITER'S DIGEST
BOOKS

WritersDigest.com
Cincinnati, Ohio

For more resources for writers, visit www.writersdigest.com/books.

17 16 15 14 13 5 4 3 2 1

Distributed in Canada by Fraser Direct
100 Armstrong Avenue
Georgetown, Ontario, Canada L7G 5S4
Tel: (905) 877-4411

Distributed in the U.K. and Europe by F+W Media International
Brunel House, Newton Abbot, Devon, TQ12 4PU, England
Tel: (+44) 1626-323200, Fax: (+44) 1626-323319
E-mail: postmaster@davidandcharles.co.uk

Distributed in Australia by Capricorn Link
P.O. Box 704, Windsor, NSW 2756 Australia
Tel: (02) 4577-3555

Edited by Rachel Randall
Designed by Claudean Wheeler
Illustrations by Sergey Kandakov/Fotolia.com
Production coordinated by Debbie Thomas

Dedication:

For my parents, who never doubted—even when I did—that I would finally publish a book.

For Mike, who encouraged me to write this one.

Acknowledgments

I hope the very pages of this book make it clear that I am deeply indebted to a number of people who shaped my writing from an early age, and by extension also helped shape this book. Thank you for all the advice, feedback, cheerleading, and reality checks. I wouldn't be in this business without you.

I would like to especially thank the friends who read portions of this book, chatted with me about it, and offered ideas that greatly improved it: Colleen Oakley, Gibson Fay-LeBlanc, Diana Renn, Terra Elan McVoy, Bradley Philbert, Kristin Zisson, Johanna Lane, Mike Harvkey, Josh Weil, Cheryl Pappas, Ivana Viani, Jason Marshall, Laura White, Ellen Spaldo, Janet Boyd, and Catherine Parilla. I also feel so grateful for, and flattered by, the support and cheers of many friends, including Lori, Wendy, Elizabeth, Laura, Shannon, and my wonderful Drop-In and book club pals (in both states!). Thanks, too, to Libby Jones, who set my mind at ease by playing with my daughter while I wrote.

Shannon Marshall—old friend, writing buddy, and YARN co-founder—in too many ways to list here, this book would not be possible without you. And you, too, Danielle Fodor—your SARK-ian belief in the power of art is always an inspiration to me. Radha Pathak—thank you for reading, and for talking me down from innumerable cliffs over the years.

Everyone on the 2012 YARN staff whom I haven't mentioned already—Lourdes, Jessica, Julia, Stephanie N. and Stephanie M., Jessica, Andrea, Mike, and Bronwyn—are such stars. Our journal runs because of all your hard work and great ideas, and I can't tell you how much I appreciate your time and enthusiasm, especially while I was also writing this book.

Let me just say again how lucky I feel to have Penn Whaling as my literary agent—Penn, you've been so steadfast in your belief in me, words and flowers don't do my gratitude justice. Ann Rittenberg, too, thanks for investing in me over the years; as I hope certain chapters convey, I really appreciate it.

Thanks, too, to Scott Francis and Phil Sexton at Writer's Digest Books, whose initial belief in TINAWM helped make this dream a reality. Rachel Randall—when you asked to remain my editor, I was so thrilled, and I have thoroughly enjoyed working with you on this process. Claudean Wheeler, your awesome cover design made me feel way cooler than I really am. Elizabeth Creehan—thank you so much for catching all those embarrassing errors. Julie Oblander—I feel like I am in such good hands!

At the risk of repeating my dedication, I can't end this section without again conveying my deep and abiding love for my family. Mike, Mom, and Dad—your unwavering belief in me has meant more to me than I can possibly convey here or in a thousand dedications. I love you guys. And Mike—thank you for reading and editing. (Seriously! Here it is in print!). Even you, Todd—I know all your teasing meant you thought having a writer for a sister was pretty cool. Susan, Jay, and Alexa—thank you so much for your words of encouragement. And little Elena—thanks for being such a good sport while Mommy wrote her book. I love you to pieces.

About the Author

Kerri Majors is the Editor and Founder of YARN, the Young Adult Review Network (www.yareview.net), an online literary journal of YA short stories, essays, and poetry, which won an Innovations in Reading Prize from the National Book Foundation. Kerri's short stories and essays have appeared in journals such as *Guernica* and *Poets and Writers*. She is a graduate of U.C. Berkeley, has an MFA from Columbia, and now lives in Massachusetts with her husband, Mike, and their daughter. You can find out more about her at www.kerrimajors.com.

TABLE OF
Contents

Introduction 1

PART I:
The Writing Process

Drafting: Buy A Planner...4

Writing Without Writing 11

Eavesdropping.. 16

Feedback..20

Revision..26

Watch Your Soap Operas..32

My First Big Mistake 37

Come At It From The Side..44

Leave Your Ego At The Door.......................................52

Play With Your Words..58

PART 2:
The Writing Life

Advice 63
The Creative Writing Major 68
Find Yourself An Audience 75
Bosom Writing Buddies 80
Workshops and Writers' Groups 84
How Good Am I?
    Or, The World Is Not A Meritocracy After All 93
It Should Be Difficult 98
In Fact, Sometimes It Will Downright Suck 105
But! "You Are Rare and Wonderous!" 110

PART 3:
Looking Ahead:
SUPPORTING YOURSELF, GETTING PUBLISHED, *and not* GETTING PUBLISHED

Is It A Hobby Or A Job? 114
Sorry, But Yes, You Do Have To "Get A Real Job" 118
Those Who Can't Do, Teach 122
Hating Your Best Friend 133

Hating Yourself 141
Writing For Pleasure 145
Getting Published, Big Time and Small Time 149
Published Writing Is A Team Effort 165
Readers Are The Best Friends
    A Writer Will Never Meet 173

Appendix (Not The One You Had Out When You Were 10) 180
Bibliography 196

INTRODUCTION

Like the title suggests, this is not a manual, textbook, guidebook, or handbook, and I would know because I have read, taught from, and written all of the above. I prefer to think of this book as therapy for writers— the kind of book I wish someone had given me when I was a younger writer, so that I would know what I was in for. Okay, so plenty of people told me what I was in for. Here's some of the wisdom I got, starting in high school, when I quit practicing my flute and piano and dedicated all my creative energies to writing:

> "I hope you're planning to marry money."
>> "Be sure to find something practical to do, because there isn't much money in writing."
>> "Grow a thick skin."
>> "You should write mysteries. I hear there's money in that."
>> "Have you thought about writing romance novels? I hear you can make lots of money with those."
>> "Nice work if you can get it."
>> "Don't quit your day job."
>> "That's a long road."

Caution, caution, caution! When people saw me, a young creative writer bursting at the seams with enthusiasm, all they wanted to talk to me about was 1) money and 2) how hard it would be to attain my goal. Although none of that advice was from actual writers—I did eventually get advice from actual writers, but I'll get to that later—I have to admit that all of it would, in fact, turn out to be true.

Yes, true.

But I hope you'll keep reading.

Because the thing is, when I was a teenager hearing all that depressing advice, I would smile and nod and say, "Thanks," even though in my mind I was thinking, "Are you crazy? You'll be eating crow when you see me on *Oprah* next year."

Fast-forward to my mid-thirties: I haven't been on *Oprah* yet and never will, since her show's gone. But I'm still writing. In fact, my entire professional life revolves around writing in one form or another, and the times I've strayed from the writing path have made me pretty unhappy.

So even though all that depressing advice about having a day job and growing a thick skin turned out to be right, I wouldn't have it any other way.

Confusing, I know. But that's why I'm writing this book: to explain to my teenage self (and any other young writers out there who are interested) why and how the writing life is worth the torture of listening to all that bummer advice and discovering that it's all true.

I'm writing this book as someone who was a teen writer with massive hopes and dreams, someone who has had some exciting successes but still hasn't landed The Big One (a book deal for a novel), and so is still very much an aspiring writer like you. I'm also writing as the editor of YARN, the Young Adult Review Network, the (ahem, ahem) award-winning YA literary journal I started because I saw a need for other writers out there. I have to admit that I'm also writing as a teacher of writing, but please don't hold that against me. It's hard to avoid, since I taught everything from composition to fiction and even poetry for eight years before I moved to Massachusetts and had a baby. But I'll try not to get all schoolmarmy on you.

I promise not to say, "You gotta have hope—just keep on keepin' on," either. You don't need that, and neither do I.

Another promise: No writing exercises. No homework. No "you have to... ."

Because remember, this is *not* a manual, textbook, or guidebook—plenty of those can be found at your local library, and I provide a bibliography with a few good ones at the end of this book so you can check them out and read them. *This* book is just you and me, in writing therapy together, so we can talk about what it means to be a writer and why the writing life is worth living.

PART 1

The WRITING PROCESS

Drafting:
BUY A PLANNER

Run, run, as fast as you can...

Those are the "It was a dark and stormy night"-esque first words of the novel I started writing in seventh grade, which was not my first attempt at a novel, mind you. My first attempt was in fifth grade, and the protagonist was a tween girl who befriended a new girl in town, only to fall in love with her older, blind brother. I wrote that first one on a yellow legal pad—or rather, the fifty-ish pages I wrote went on a yellow legal pad. Two years later, I got much more professional and used my dad's computer. This was 1987, so you've got to picture a big spoiled-cream-colored box with a black screen and blinking green cursor. *Awesome.* I saved the chapters on floppy disks and printed them on a dot matrix printer; I had to rip the perforated strips off the continuous form paper, which always gave me paper cuts.

The novel that I began in seventh grade was about a girl and her guy friend who become renegades, on the run from some big, scary, menacing ... Well, I couldn't figure that out at first. I wasn't the type to run away from home myself, and neither were any of my friends. Life was just too comfortable with our braces, Walkmans, and snacks from Costco. I only had *21 Jump Street* to inform me about the kind of teen angst that might cause a smart young woman with loving parents to run, run as fast as she could. Also, I was a big fan of *West Side Story*, so I fear my novel was a bit derivative. I eventually decided that my characters should be in trouble with a gang; I'm pretty sure it was the guy's fault, and that the heroine was just being a loyal, but clearly crushing, friend. Oh yes, if I'd ever finished this novel—or ever been kissed that year, for that matter—kissing would have ensued.

But kissing didn't ensue, for her or for me, in the months I spent working on that (still, alas, unfinished) novel. Working up to that kiss produced quite a number of pages, however, and it garnered me my first honest-to-goodness audience (see "Find Yourself an Audience"). It was the first time I realized that if I, the writer, was producing pages in excited anticipation of an event (kissing or being caught by the authorities while on the run with her crush), then likely my readers would be as well. I also discovered that sometimes you have to make the sexy hero do something bad. At some point, I realized that in order for the story to move forward and for the protagonist to have something to grapple with, I had to allow the guy friend to accidentally kill someone.

So, writing this novel taught me a great deal about characters and how a writer is supposed to move them around on the page, coaxing them into doing what is needed from them. There was a lot of deleting and moving around of words and sentences in each of my sessions in front of the computer. As I wrote, I kept discovering new things about my two characters and realizing that things I'd written about them ten pages earlier couldn't possibly be true because I had just realized these new things about their personalities.

Ah, the pleasures and surprises of writing a first draft.

Like many writers, I love drafting. It feels a lot like a joyride with friends. I am aware, of course, that many other writers fear drafting. They get hung up on the legitimate problems of self-censorship, writer's block, fear, procrastination, and a whole host of other pathologies endemic to the profession, which I discuss elsewhere in this book.

In a moment of crazy serendipity as I was revising this very chapter, I took a little procrastination break and checked Facebook, only to see that a published-novelist friend had posted something quite interesting about drafting. In response to a link he shared that contained an essay about revision, he wrote:

> "I have to say that I disagree with the fundamental concept: that 'revision is where we do our most important work as writers.' Though that seems to have become a favorite saying among teachers of writing (precisely because it's the easiest part to teach). It might be where we spend a lot of time, and it might be where we do really hard work (I've spent years of hard work rewriting my latest project), but I still believe the most important work—the stuff that makes revision worth it—comes in that initial writing, the first draft. Hard as it is to face that (precisely because it's a whole lot harder to come up with a list of tools to work on something that in many ways springs from the subconscious)."

Perhaps that's so, and for some writers more than others. Drafting, he implies, is essentially gut work, and I agree with him. Not only does it take guts to write a *draft*, sometimes in defiance of parents who want you to be a doctor or a world that tells you the odds are against you, a writer also tends to draft from his gut, from that intuitive writer's part of him that speaks, frequently, at inconvenient times (1 a.m.?), of inconvenient things (of those parents, maybe, or a lost love). Most people's guts don't take well to being shaped by tools. Guts are inherently wild and free. When you're writing, they do their best work unbridled.

As Anne Lamott will be happy to remind you in her classic chapter "Shitty First Drafts," from her life-changing writing book *Bird by Bird*, "The only way I can get anything written is to write really, really shitty first drafts ... The first draft is the child's draft, where you let it all pour out and romp all over the place, knowing that no one is going to see it and you can shape it later." So remember, no one has to see that first draft! You can say anything you want! The whole point of a first draft is to get it all out. Gush those guts onto the blank, white page. Go ahead. Don't self-censor. Just say it. You can fix, edit, delete, and finesse it later.

That's exactly what I learned to do during all those afternoons in junior high spent writing my crappy novel about two runaways. I wrote because I loved writing, and in the process I learned a lot about how to write better. I could make a long list of what I learned from writing that book, but most of those lessons were highly specific to the project and not especially relevant here. This book isn't so much about making you a better writer with the goal of getting you published—there are plenty of those on the market (see the bibliography)—as it is about helping you live your life as a writer. There is a difference. So the following recollection about my own drafting is much more to the point.

I have always tried to write every day.

I often worked on that runaways novel after school. I would walk home from Morada Middle School and eat an after-school snack: chips, cookies, or maybe some fruit or celery sticks with peanut butter if my mother intervened. Snack consumed and blood sugar appropriately elevated, I would head to the back room of the house closest to the garage, which smelled a bit like dried dog food and housed my father's fly-fishing equipment and home gym in addition to his desktop computer, where I would type away for ... I want to say hours at a time, but I doubt that's true. Maybe an hour to an hour and a half each time.

Sometimes I would work on the novel after dinner when the sun had gone down. I loved working when it was dark. Gloomy, rainy afternoons also put me in the mood to write. Darkness made me feel pleasantly trapped with my characters, which helped me better feel their emotions and envision where *they* were. I suspect this is how a lot of writers feel about their 2 a.m. writing sessions, a oneness with the draft made possible by the sensation that only he and his characters are awake, and in this thing together. (I'm more of a daytime writer these days since that's when my brain works best, though I have been known to get up in the middle of the night or early in the morning if I've been woken by some annoying thing that forces my mind to drift to whatever I've been writing lately. Sometimes the muse won't let me sleep, and I have to get up.)

And yet, despite my preference for dark and gloomy writing conditions, I wrote my middle school novel on sunny days as well. I wrote pretty much every day.

This is important. Sitting down every day, or most days, to write will help you get your draft done.

In my twenty-six years of creative writing (counting from fifth grade and that first novel), I discovered that many of my peers would *only* sit down to face a draft under specific circumstances: dark and gloomy, after midnight, on vacation, three hours before a deadline, when the moon was waning and not waxing, when their tarot card reader told them the conditions were ideal. You get my point. Over the years, it became clear to me that those writers weren't producing as many pages as I was. Oh, they would often produce far more pages in one sitting—especially the three-hours-before-a-deadline writers—but overall, my novel pages were stacking up in a pretty impressive way.

Remember that annoying tale of the tortoise and the hare your grandparents used to regale you with? It turns out to be true. And it's one of the only things professional writers seem to have in common: They know that drafting is a daily discipline. Revising and editing are, too, but I'll get to those later.

Daily discipline doesn't have to mean you write every single day. It does mean this for some writers, but it hasn't for me, at least not in more recent years. It really means something closer to weekly discipline. Let me explain.

When I wrote my third novel—my first official *finished* novel—the year after I graduated from college, I did write nearly every day of the work week. I orchestrated my whole life around my writing schedule, working for money as a nanny and a bookstore clerk with flexible hours. In the mornings, I wrote for at least two hours each day. When I took a job managing an olive oil shop, my writing schedule was derailed; I had to work significantly more hours, and my mornings were no longer protected. Starting grad school helped a bit, but I lost my sense of routine, and the addition of teaching in grad school only made the time crunch worse. It seemed I was spending all my time reading for discussion seminars or prepping and grading for the classes I was teaching. Plus, I wanted to have a *life*. I lived in New York City for goodness sake. There were restaurants and museums to go to!

I had forgotten that a routine was exactly what I needed to meet the deadlines in my MFA* classes and ultimately produce my thesis. The reason I was in grad school in the first place was, after all, to *be a writer*. It took my then-boyfriend/now-husband Mike to say to me something like, "You need to plan out a weekly schedule for your writing," for me to realize that what was keeping me from being a writer wasn't my teaching or my social life. No, I had a time-management problem.

Since I am a great seeker of advice, I went looking for best practices. I talked to a former professor and a good friend, both of whom are writers in their own ways. They're not novelists or poets, but like many people in not-apparently-writing professions, professors and lawyers have to write *a ton*, just as much as many creative writers in fact. This writing, in addition to the teaching and lawyering, actually pays their rents. Both my friends commiserated about how hard it was to fit writing into a busy work and social life, and how they, too, had lost their ways to their drafts in the past. But they gave me the exact same advice as my boyfriend had: "You need to make a schedule and stick to it." To help me do that seemingly simple thing, they recommended time-management books (*The Clockwork Muse* by Eviatar Zerubavel and *Time Management from the Inside Out* by Julie Morgenstern, both in the bibliography) that truly got me out of the predicament I was in.

It turned out I had to buy a better planner and actually write down specific times each week that I planned to write. The more regular my writing sessions, the less chance I had of getting distracted from the story at hand.

---

*An MFA is a Master of Fine Arts. This is a master's degree in the study of a particular art. Mine is in writing, with a concentration in fiction, but you can also get MFAs in theater, visual arts, and film.

Miraculously, I still got everything else done—the grading, the prepping, and all the other stuff that had been ballooning out of control to fill up my every hour. As a bonus, I got faster and more efficient at many tasks, because *I had to*. Without the incentive to write for those six hours every week, I probably never would have reduced the time I spent grading one paper from an *hour* to twenty minutes, without damaging my effectiveness as a teacher.

True, as I got older and more responsibilities demanded my time, I would have to give up some things in order to protect those precious hours in my week reserved for writing. Gym sessions became shorter, dinners I cooked became less complicated. I went out a little less so that I could be fresh and prepared to face those pages in the morning. But as I got older, it also became more and more apparent to me that I was never going to become a writer unless I protected my schedule. Without the time, there would be no pages. Without the pages, there would be no book deal. The only difference between now and then is that my calendar is online instead of on paper, and I feel like I'm doing the earth a favor.

In junior high, drafting every day had been a pleasure, my "me time" away from schoolwork, mean girls, and he-loves-me-he-loves-me-not concerns.

It still is my me time today. I just had to figure out how to make it happen again.

WRITING
Without WRITING*

*Y*ou know those moments when you *know* you should be writing, but you're just so tired or otherwise fried you're not sure you can put one word in front of the other? I've had plenty of those days. When I'm supposed to be writing and I don't feel like it, the conversation in my head usually goes something like this:

I could do laundry. I could do dishes. I could nap.

I could write.

Or nap.

Write.

Nap.

No, Kerri, really you should be writing.

Ah, yes. Writing. That thing I'm supposed to be doing. Because I'm a writer. If I'm not writing, how can I call myself a writer at all?

But at one in the afternoon, after getting up with a toddler at five in the morning, the thought of writing seems, well, exhausting. But I *have* to write. If I don't write, I will lose all respect for myself, and all contact with the story I've been working away at.

---

*An earlier version of this chapter appeared as a blog on YARN (http://yareview.net/2011/04/writing-without-writing).

Then I remember that I have to do some reading before I can really move forward with my story.

Reading, I sigh with relief. Yes, reading I can do. Feeling a surge of energy, I grab myself a cup of tea so I can settle down under a blanket on the couch with the book in question. *That's* more like it!

When I'm reading, I *am* writing. This is a more obvious connection when the reading is directly related to the writing project. That kind of reading is research, and writers have to do it all the time at varying degrees of intensity. Some writers have a love-hate relationship with research. At one of the first lectures I attended at Columbia, Mark Slouka, one of the eminent fiction writers on the faculty, was discussing research, and I'll never forget what he said about it: "It's better just to get in and get out as soon as you can." He thought that lingering too long over your research could stall your story, or worse, make it stale and textbook-like.

Not so for many other writers, especially those who write historical fiction like Jennifer Donnelly or Dorothy Hearst, both of whom told YARN much about the pleasures of researching their books. Donnelly revealed that for her novels, which are anything but stale, "No amount of research is enough. If there were no such things as deadlines, I'd still be researching for *Revolution*! I research before I start, as I'm working, when I'm editing and proofreading, and right up until my editor says, 'Give it here! Now!'"

Dorothy Hearst, author of *Promise of the Wolves* and *Secrets of the Wolves*, wrote an entire essay for YARN descriptively titled "How I Went from Hating Research to Loving It." She makes research sound breathtakingly adventurous: "In the course of my research, I chased huskies through the French Alps, braved negative 40-degree weather in Yellowstone, watched wolves feeding a few hundred yards away from me, and walked through caves where someone else had stood 14,000 years ago painting bison and horses on the stone wall." I'll buy a ticket for that trip, please.

And to think that all that exciting reading about people and places far away from your desk counts as writing. You can even do it with your feet up or in a nice, cool library if you can't afford air conditioning in your first apartment.

I've always been one for taking notes on my research as I read. If I own the book, I do it right on the page, underlining sentences I like and jotting down responses in the margins. If I don't own it, I'll type notes into a computer or jot them down in a notebook. Okay, so note-taking makes my reading sound more like actual writing than writing without writing, but it doesn't *feel* that way. Since I'm responding to what I'm reading, somehow the process doesn't feel as arduous. I'm not creating something from nothing.

When you're a writer, research isn't the only kind of reading that counts as writing. Reading for your English or creative writing class? Definitely writing—especially because you're going to discuss it in class and thus learn something about the way it was written that you can apply to your own work. The case is the same for reading a novel for a book club. Reading for your editing job is similar, too; for me, at least, the process of editing is intimately related to the process of writing.

Virtually all reading, even reading for pure pleasure, can count as writing if you want to think of it that way. As long as you ask yourself during or after reading, "Why did I like that so much?" Or even, "Why did I stop liking it on page 230?" Or, "Why did it drag in the middle, then get better again?" Or, "Why didn't the rest of the book live up to the promise of the first chapter?" If you're asking these or any other craft-related questions the book poses for you, then, my friend, you are writing. Of course, you also have to answer the questions. Every time you do, you are learning more about the craft of writing. And that's essential to becoming a better writer.

This is all true in a general sense, but more specifically, it's been while reading that I've had some accidental but major breakthroughs with my own writing. Countless times I've been stuck in my own writing—maybe a character isn't as interesting anymore, or the plot is stalled, or I can't seem to let a character do what she needs to do. A few days later, I'll be reading, reading, reading a novel I picked up for fun, and something in that book will spark my imagination, then *hey, presto!* I have a solution to the problem in my own writing.

All this talking somewhat irreverently about reading as a tool for my writing makes it easy to forget that reading is where my writing began. It began on a summer day when I picked up Louisa May Alcott's *Little Women* and couldn't put it down; on afternoons in fifth grade when I would chill out with the cooler-than-me chicks from *Sweet Valley High*; during my first week at college when someone handed me her favorite novel, *Possession* by A.S. Byatt, and told me I *had* to read it. She was so right. I did have to read it, because reading Byatt would forever change the course of my own writing. (Since I don't want to repeat myself, have a look at "The Creative Writing Major" later in this book for more on my Byatt love.)

The first two novels that truly exerted their influence on me as a writer, causing me to reconsider the way I wrote, were Ken Follett's *Pillars of the Earth* and Marion Zimmer Bradley's *The Mists of Avalon*, both of which I read in the summers around my junior year of high school. If you're familiar with those novels, you'll probably infer from them that I was a bit of an early English history buff in high school. And yes, I admit, I even went to a Renaissance fair. (I'm letting it all hang out in this book.)

Pillars of the Earth showed me that complexity and fun could actually coexist in the same novel. Not only is Follett's novel full of Wild West-style violence and feuding, it also contains several heartbreaking and sexy romances. It is densely and lushly plotted over many decades, giving the full scope of the lives of many characters and their families, all of whom are focused in one way or another on the building of a cathedral in twelfth-century England. Full of researched details about homes and food and dress from the time period, it is also chockablock with architectural history and engineering. Not only was I utterly swept away by the story, I learned a great deal as I read. Before this novel, I had never really thought it was possible to marry entertainment and learning in one novel. It wasn't that I thought it was *impossible*; it's just that I hadn't thought about doing it at all.

The Mists of Avalon reinforced this notion that literature can be both transporting and educational. Bradley's novel isn't as learned as Follett's per se, but I could tell that she'd done a great deal of reading and thinking about Arthurian legends and early Christianity in order to come up with her own version of the story of King Arthur.

Because of her novel, I wound up reading Thomas Mallory and other early Arthurian texts, which weren't nearly as enjoyable as *Avalon* but taught me much about England, myths, and legends. Plus, because of reading *Avalon*, I told my mom I was going to have to stop going to church.

My mother and I had a couple of big fights about this choice during my senior year. I was raised Catholic, and before reading *Avalon*, I had certainly clued in to the fact that the church had a long and ongoing history of oppression of many kinds (*Pillars* helped with this impression as well), and that maybe, just maybe, its beliefs weren't any more valid than those of the pagan hoards it sought to bloodily subjugate. *Avalon* crystallized much of what I'd already been thinking, and its rebellious, tenacious heroine Morgaine inspired me to be more like her.

Those books and many that followed changed me as a writer and as a person. By showing me what was possible within the binding of a book, they opened my eyes to expansive and poignant possibilities for literature and—at the risk of sounding corny—humanity.

So read. And don't feel guilty for taking time from the computer or from anything else to do it.

EAVESDROPPING

Though I'm sure none of my mother's friends who are reading this book will be glad to read this, I was an inveterate eavesdropper as a kid. I listened to every conversation I could get my ears on. The messier and juicier, the better.

But I'd like to wholeheartedly *thank* all the people whose traumas shaped my writing and worldview, because my perspective wouldn't be nearly as complex or interesting without my clandestine observations.

Don't worry, I'm not going to name names (sorry, readers!) or even get particularly specific about what I learned. In fact, some of you will be delighted to know that I've actually forgotten who did what to whom. We're talking about data that's fifteen to twenty-five years old, and I listened to a lot of conversations outside as well as inside my home, so at some point the whos, hows, whens, and wheres began to blur, partly because the events didn't happen directly to me. But by the time I started college, I'd heard an earful about the world of adult woes: precious information about divorces, firings, drugs, booze, filial spite, heirlooms, and on and on—and not just the events themselves, but also the emotional fallouts from them, as well as the kinds of advice that got doled out in response.

Did all that information make me a prescient, precocious writer?

Not really. In fact, if anything, it made me a worse writer for a little while when I was trying to write about things that had never happened to me, things above my head that I'd had no real experience with. But every writer needs to reach, and reach I did. My first completed novel, which I wrote after college but actually started kicking around in high school, was about a mother who leaves her daughter to be raised by her own dysfunctional parents. It's told from the point of view of the mother, the grandmother, and the abandoned daughter who is college age during the events of the book. The abandoned girl's grandfather, who is in some ways the central character of the book, is dead, and it's his death that sets in motion the events of the novel.

Had I had personal experience with anything even remotely approaching these traumas? Nope. Had I eavesdropped on a conversation about any of these events? Also no.

But the eavesdropping was absolutely responsible for that novel, because what I really learned from eavesdropping, and what remains today, is a general sense of the vast moral grayness of human experience, a sense that there are few, if any, black and white, good or bad choices or people. Which, I tend to think, is the kind of thinking that leads to more interesting writing. Ambiguity is at the heart of most worthwhile fiction—consider Nick Carraway, the slippery, unreliable narrator of *The Great Gatsby*, or the brilliant but morbidly obsessed and drug-addicted Sherlock Holmes, or the violence at the heart of *Lord of the Flies*.

Okay, so my first completed novel wasn't a bestseller. In fact, it didn't even sell.

However, it did, in a roundabout way, get me my agent. Okay, really quick, since this isn't exactly the point of this chapter: When I was writing the book, I was doing a few hours of work a week for Ann Rittenberg, a literary agent who later read the book and offered some good feedback about my writing. She was intrigued enough by that novel to be open to reading more of my writing over the years, and—happy ending!—her associate Penn Whaling wound up reading my mystery novel almost ten years later and offering to represent me.

The point is this: The conversations you hear at the tops of stairs and through closed doors probably aren't going to directly result in a specific book. They *will* teach you about the world, however, and help you formulate your own ideas about how people behave and why, and *that* is priceless raw material for every writer.

Eavesdropping will teach you one explicit writing lesson, though: It'll teach you about how people talk.

Once you get over your initial shock about who's doing what to whom, you can start to focus on the words: *how* people reveal this information to friends, strangers, and enemies. You'll hear a huge variety in tones of voice and sentence structure, and you'll note many kinds of pauses, sighs, and stutters, as well as body language (if you are within sight and not behind a door with your ear to a glass). The writer in you might even start to narrate the visuals of the conversation if you can't actually see the scene unfolding, filling in the inevitable blanks left by eavesdropping. When you sit down at your computer to write your own dialogue, you'll learn to edit out the "ums" and "hrms" that are an integral part of live oral speech but heavily bog down written, edited speech.

Dialogue turns out to be phenomenally difficult to write well. I obsess over it when I'm drafting and revising. And I'll toot my own horn here for a sec: Of all the many criticisms I've received on my writing, "crappy dialogue" hasn't been a repeat offender. I'm one-hundred percent convinced I have eavesdropping to thank for this. If you listen to enough conversations, you can train your inner ear to hear how people talk. It's like listening to classical music or jazz when you want to be a musician.

Of course, this also means that when you do read crappy dialogue, your inner ear will shriek in protest. But that's really a small price to pay, isn't it?

Speaking of reading, part of what makes reading good dialogue, or any good literature, such a pleasure is that it feels like eavesdropping, doesn't it? You get to be a fly on the wall for all those juicy, messy times when the you-know-what hits the fan: last words to estranged children who come home for the final hand holding, shouting matches between girlfriends and boyfriends and (if you're lucky) the makeup sex after the fight, what really happened to the little brother after he disappeared that hot summer afternoon.

Great reads are full of secrets revealed. It's never too late for a writer to start collecting them.

FEEDBACK

When I was in high school, one of the best things I did for my writing was join the speech and debate team. Here's a quick primer for those of you who don't know about your school's speech team (or who might be thinking about joining, which I highly recommend). As the name suggests, the team is made up of 1) debaters who can do a variety of types of debate from solo to team to "Congress" style, and 2) "speechies" who can compete in a variety of styles of speech, from Dramatic or Humorous Interpretation (DI and HI, in which the speechie acts out a ten-minute piece of a play, movie, or novel), to Original Oratory (for which the speechie writes and performs a ten-minute speech on a particular topic). Competitions are held on Saturdays at regional high schools, and larger, longer invitational tournaments are held at college campuses over entire weekends.

Though I had done very well outside the weekend circuit in the Lions-Club-sponsored oratory contests, my real category—the one that defined me and made me feel like a real writer—was OPP, Original Prose and Poetry, for which competitors wrote a short story of about five pages and performed it in less than ten minutes. I remember very distinctly what it felt like to write first drafts of stories and speeches for the speech team: When it was going well, I got this tingly feeling in the lower right corner of my back. Because I'd been thinking about the character and story for a while before sitting down at the computer, the whole thing would usually gush out in one sitting, and I would get completely swept up in the emotions of the piece. Where appropriate, I wiped away a tear or laughed out loud.

Yeah, I thought I was hot stuff.

At the first speech meetings I attended in my freshman year, I heard from the upperclassmen that the coach enjoyed ripping his students' writing to shreds, but that it made them all better writers. Though I recoiled at the phrase "rip to shreds," I was comforted by the camaraderie and jokey rapport between this seemingly good-natured but very sarcastic, balding, mustachioed man and the juniors and seniors who obviously liked him so much. Plus, it wasn't like I was a stranger to feedback. I had shared pages from my first and second attempts at novels with my sixth grade and junior high English teachers, and both of them had offered compliments and suggestions for improvement.

I wasn't quite prepared, though, for what hit me during that first speech practice when I read aloud my first-ever OPP story. The speech team met in the evenings—the coach was a school administrator who came to the high school after his day job at the district office—and it was dark outside. I was one of several freshmen who came to read and get initial comments on our speeches. The coach had assured us ahead of time that since we were all newbies, we wouldn't be subjected to the sometimes unkind remarks of the upperclassmen who thought they knew everything but didn't.

The first reader of the night—not me, thankfully—began with an apology: "I'm really sorry, but this isn't as good as I'd like it to be..."

At which point the coach interrupted and said, "Never apologize for your work. If I was about to put on a production of *Hamlet* and started by apologizing for not rehearsing enough, would you want to stay and watch?"

Point taken.

As I listened to the coach deliver feedback to a few speechies before me, I started to relax. He wasn't that bad. Honest, yes, but he knew what he was talking about. I agreed with everything he was saying. Still, he hadn't yet heard any original writing; he'd only been hearing interpretations.

When it was my turn, I read my piece nervously and without apologies, but also full of excited anticipation. I was pretty sure it was good, since it was a reworking of a story I'd written to some accolades in eighth grade. I was encouraged by the genuinely warm smile on the coach's face and the anticipatory, hunched-forward postures of the other freshmen in the room. When I was finished, I heaved a sigh of relief.

He—and everyone else, not that they mattered in that moment—raised his hands to clap while he continued to smile. Did I see something to the effect of *this girl's going all the way to State* in his expression? I thought so, tentatively. What I mainly felt was relieved that I hadn't made a total fool of myself.

Opening his arms to the room of my peers, the coach asked, "What did you think?" He'd opened the floor like this for all the previous speeches.

Some solid compliments set me at ease, especially when he agreed with what he heard.

Then he asked if anyone had any suggestions.

As I later learned was typical in a room full of apprehensive young writer-actor-artists, no one had any.

"Well," said the coach, still smiling, "I have a few suggestions. But we'll get to those later." He looked at his watch. "It's getting late! I don't want your parents getting angry at me on the first night."

What?

Later?

When?

Was it so bad he couldn't give me the two or three tips he'd thrown at the others?

The room dissolved into a buzz of reassured self-congratulation. We'd all survived!

Maybe.

I lingered until I was one of the last students left in the classroom, so I could wander over to the coach and ask, "Was it that bad?"

He gave me an indulgent but slightly exasperated smile—an expression I would learn was an ironic form of affection, like the smiles you get from a favorite uncle who loves you right back—and said, "What did I say about apologizing?"

"But I wasn't—"

"You're doubting your work."

I wasn't sure how to respond, so I didn't.

"Are *you* proud of your work?"

"Yes," I said, not at all sure if that was the truth anymore.

"Then it doesn't really matter what I think. I'm here to help you make what *you* do as good as it can be."

"Will you give me comments? Help?"

"Sure," he said, as if he could take it or leave it. "When can you come back?"

We negotiated a time. I returned. And I got awesome feedback. Every single time. For four years, and then after high school as well.

Feedback from the coach always felt more like a jam session than a critique. He'd get really excited about the parts he liked and ask me to read them over and over, and then he'd ask me questions to get me to do *more* of that thing I was doing so well. This was all done tutorially, in a conversation. The "rip to shreds" rumor I'd heard might have felt true to some writers, since our sessions did usually result in major changes to my first draft. But I found our conversations exhilarating—I *wanted* to get better. Afterward, I'd hurry home and make the changes we'd talked about.

And that's pretty much how it went for the next four years. I'd write a short story or an oratory and bounce into speech practice, where I'd get the compliments of friends and the balanced critique of a pro. Writers always need both.

Whenever I teach creative writing, especially to scared beginning writers, I always encourage them to give their writing to their mother/spouse/sibling/anyone who will be inclined to find the *most* positive things about it. Because writing is *hard*. You're insecure about it. You might even be well aware that it sucks. If you're going to soldier on, you need to be told that it's good, and why it's good. Especially because when you hand it over to the pro who knows what he's talking about, you just might want to cry.

This is controversial advice. Many writers would tell you to avoid the inexperienced readers who will be almost uniformly positive because they don't know what they are talking about, artistically speaking, and their praise might artificially inflate your ego and become a talisman against the more correct, but far harsher, feedback of the pro.

There is some truth to that advice, but if you're *aware* that the first type of feedback is going to be hyperbolically complimentary, then you're not likely to run into the problem. Think of the first feedback as fortification, not inoculation. Enjoy the praise like you would a secret bowl of ice cream, then sit down and take your medicine.

I use the term *pro* loosely here by the way. For me, in high school, the coach was my pro. So was my American history teacher, who was also the faculty moderator of the high school newspaper, who taught me just as much about researching and crafting a good essay as the coach taught me about shaping a compelling story. As time went on, many of my classmates and fellow competitors from other schools also became pros: experienced peer writers who thought a lot about the craft of writing and respected me and my work enough to give me the honest feedback I needed.

This is the theory behind writing workshops: Put ten or so writers in a class together with a teacher, and they will give each other plenty of feedback to help improve everyone's writing. In classes I took with writers I liked and respected, I learned as much if not more from my peers as I did from my teachers, especially when I saw that you got as good as you gave. In other words, if you write thoughtful comments on someone else's work, they are much more likely to write thoughtful comments on yours. One of the greatest writerly compliments I ever received was when the coach gave me his poetry to read after I'd graduated from high school. He respected my writing enough to want *my* feedback.

All this is true even though you'll probably only use about five percent of the feedback you hear. Well, let me amend that: The five percent rule comes from the world of MFA workshops, where writers are older and more experienced than I was in high school. Early in high school, I think I incorporated about fifty percent of what I heard from the coach and other teachers, and about ten percent of what I heard from my friends. By the time I graduated it was probably closer to twenty percent and five percent, respectively. After all, hearing and using the feedback for revision is an art and not a science; it's hard to quantify. I'm just giving you these numbers as a general guide to serve as a reminder that you don't have to weight all feedback equally, nor do you have to blindly accept all the feedback you receive.

By the time I got to college, I saw that delivering feedback on others' writing served yet another purpose: It helped me form and articulate my own literary tastes.

For instance, in a fiction workshop I took as an undergrad, I discovered I really didn't like "sketches" or "slice of life" stories—the kinds of whimsical pieces in which a character would be in a car, listening to Tracy Chapman, thinking about how much his life sucked. I liked *plot*. Something had to happen, and preferably get resolved, for me to become invested. In school, it was a revelation to discover that not everyone liked plot. Some writers, notably the ones toting around books by Don DeLillo or Jorge Luis Borges, thought that *plot* was an inferior concern for serious writers. For them, plot was on par with *Sesame Street*. *Language* was the higher art, on par with Picasso. I'm not getting into that debate here. It's not important what you like; it *is* important to learn how to implement what you like. Knowing what you like and don't like—and *why*—is key to learning to write what you like, and do it well.

Giving, receiving, and hearing loads of feedback let me in on these esoteric writerly concerns and made me into a convert, a believer in the power of feedback to transform my writing into words that are worthwhile. Lest you think feedback is only for the newbie, take down the latest novels of a couple of your favorite writers and read the Acknowledgments pages. You'll no doubt see heartfelt thanks to all the people who read drafts and offered feedback.

Which reminds me! Don't forget to thank your readers. They are doing you a big favor. When I feel flush, I take mine out to lunch. When I feel poor, I make them lunch. And I'm always available to read in return. It's a virtuous circle, nourishing in more ways than one.

REVISION

I have a confession to make, which I hesitate to write because it is just too cutely ironic for this chapter. Still, it must be done: I had to completely throw out and rewrite my draft of this chapter about revision. It hurt to do it, even though when I wrote the draft, I suspected it wasn't the greatest chapter ever. I knew that it wasn't quite holding together, but I followed my own advice from the drafting chapter and didn't self-censor. This unfortunately meant that I filled the draft with soapbox platitudes and, worse, schoolmarmish finger pointing. That's not what I said this book was going to be all about!

This was hardly the first time I had to face a complete do-over. I once threw out an entire novel draft and started again from scratch. It wasn't that the novel—or the first draft of this chapter for that matter—didn't contain great material. There were finely crafted sentences, scenes with snappy dialogue, three-dimensional characters. The problem was that altogether it just wasn't working. No forest existed, despite many alluring trees.

Part of what I find comforting when I *do* throw out such a large amount of material is that it lives on in my computer. I always save the draft as is and start a new document for the rewrite. That way I am not *losing* it exactly, and if I want to import a section from the draft, all I have to do is cut and paste. I do something similar for smaller-scale revisions: While I'm working to revise the draft, I open a file called "Cuts" where I can cut and paste lines that I really like but aren't doing enough work in the piece at hand. Occasionally, those cuts become essays or stories of their own.

You're probably starting to glean from my descriptions of revision that I'm not talking about proofreading here. Proofreading, which consists of checking your prose for spelling and grammar errors and stylistic consistency, is an extremely important final step before you hand in that story or send out that novel to agents. But it's just that: a *final* step. Revision is much messier, because it requires you to really listen to all that feedback from friends, pros, and the little writer's voice in your own head telling you the draft isn't working, and figure out how to apply it to your draft. This is a painstaking and painful process—which is why, I suspect, so many writers resist revision.

I've been there.

In my third MFA workshop, when I heard my peers' comments on my latest story boiling down to, "Show more, tell less," I just about lost it in front of the class. I felt—and looked—like I wanted to hurl the pages across the room and yell my head off. I'd heard this *so many times before*. For years! Years! Since, like, *middle school*.

I just barely managed to contain my anger when I asked, "*Where* am I telling? It *feels* like I'm showing. All over the place." The pages of my story were careworn and slightly damp from my sweaty palms and fidgety fingers. I knew my irritation was obvious in my voice, and I didn't care, even though I always tried to cultivate a certain nonchalance in these critique classes.

The teacher, one I really admired for her calm manner, practical advice, and her way of never playing favorites with the students, intervened and said to me, "Well, one example is on page 3 where you explain to us why the character is in trouble instead of showing us his trouble through action."

"But that's just two paragraphs," I pressed. "There's action on the next page. Am I not allowed to tell at all?"

I am not exactly sure what the teacher said in that white-knuckle moment in class. The fact that I was hearing this "show, don't tell" comment on my writing drove me nuts not just because I'd been hearing it forever, but because 1) plenty of writers told as much if not more than they showed (hello, people ... Philip Roth?), so why couldn't I? and 2) I thought I showed plenty. I'd been working on changing this so-called problem for years. Why didn't my peers get what I was trying to do?

Whatever she said to me in class was much less important than what she said over coffee and toast about a week later. After class, privately, she invited me to meet her at her favorite breakfast place early one morning for café con leche, where she listened patiently while I expressed my frustration with hearing "show, don't tell" again and again. I said I thought it was a natural prejudice of writers in workshops to think this, and that I thought my writing wasn't getting a fair shot.

Then she said, kindly but firmly, "You can tell the hell out of any story you want, as long as it's *working*. What you're hearing is that your telling isn't working. Not as well as your scenes. You write good dialogue. When your characters interact with each other on the page, we can see them and hear them. We want more of that."

So there it was. My telling sucked—at least compared to Philip Roth's. My showing was good, better than my telling. It wasn't that I *couldn't* tell; there was no rule against it. It was that I, Kerri, was better off showing. It wasn't that my peers didn't "get" my writing; it was that I didn't "get" what they were telling me.

No one had put it to me this way before.

It wasn't fun to hear. But because I respected my teacher enormously, and because I had been hearing this comment way too often, it finally sunk in. I didn't have to do everything I'd been hearing my peers tell me (recall the five percent guide from the last chapter), but I did have to fix *this*.

It was only then that I was able to roll up my sleeves and do the kind of down-and-dirty revising that not only cleaned up that one story but improved my writing overall. It was also then that I learned that all effective revision starts with respect and pattern recognition. Sometimes, no matter how hair-pullingly frustrating you find the feedback, if you're hearing it from many different people, it's a pattern. If it's a pattern, and/or if it's coming from someone you respect greatly, it's probably time to accept the advice and apply it to your writing.

I wish I could go through a list of critiques you're likely to hear about your own writing and tell you how to address them, but I can't, because your way of addressing them might be way better than mine. Everyone is different. Plus, remember that my goal in this book is to help you stay on the long road of the writing life, and with that in mind, I think it's more useful to tell you that you are not alone if you're having difficulty accepting and applying feedback. Nor are you in a camp of two (you and me); we are in very, very good company. I'll invite you over for a party one day, and you can hear one of my friends complain about how he finally had to make his protagonists less passive, or how another friend had to add a fourth section to what had been a nicely symmetric triptych-style novel, or how my playwright friend had to take the poetry out of her plays and start writing poetry instead—all because each of them were hearing feedback from respected sources that finally formed a pattern they couldn't ignore.

The good news is that these days in my fiction I rarely tell too much. I lay down scene after scene, with dialogue and action in each, like I'm laying down tracks for a train. One scene at a time. This kind of writing is hard for me; my natural inclination is to tell. Sometimes I still start to do it, but now because I'm more practiced, I can recognize when I'm telling. The same goes for a few other key weaknesses in my writing. I nip them in the bud and make adjustments as I write that first draft.

That level of self-awareness in my drafting never would have been possible without thousands of pages of revisions. And hey, I still have to do major revisions—like with this chapter—because I still bump up against new problems in my writing. That's why writers tend to call writing a *process*. It's ever evolving. If it wasn't, it would get boring.

Now when I'm in the mood to tell, I write an essay, where telling is welcome and even expected, and my telling style has gotten me more props than it did in my fiction. Discovering essay writing was an important moment in my writing development. Oh sure, I'd written essays for school, the newspaper, and those oratories on the speech team. But as a creative writer, I hadn't done much nonfiction writing. Even so, I had so much telling in me! I had to put it somewhere—and I did.

Have I convinced you to take a deep breath and go back to that story your teacher told you needed two fewer characters and a lot more dialogue?

No?

Okay, at the risk of getting back on that soapbox that I had to chuck out with my first draft of this chapter, I feel like I'd be doing you a disservice if I didn't share a few harsh realities about revision.

In college especially, I used to hear people brag about how they got *A*s on papers they had written in two hours the night before. In my MFA years, if I'd had a penny for every time I heard the following conversation, I'd be a wealthy woman:

> "I can't believe everyone liked it so much," a writer says of her draft and the workshop discussion of that draft. "I hardly spent any time on it at all."
>
> "Yeah," someone chimes in, "That always happens to me. The stuff I slave over for hours, and rework and tinker with, always gets the worst comments. And the stuff I dash off really fast before class gets the praise."
>
> "Me too!" says another writer.

Those conversations, and the *A*s so many naturally talented writers receive on papers written hastily the night before they are due, go a long way toward convincing writers that they don't need to revise their writing and that somehow their draft is sacred and should not be tampered with.

But I listened carefully in those classes where first drafts were lauded and heard plenty of suggestions alongside the praise. Perhaps the workshop comments were generally more positive than negative (it frequently goes the other way, as you can imagine), but it's not like the draft was perfect. It still needed work.

Now that I'm friends with many writers, I know that the serious ones, the ones who are now seeing their work in print, didn't take those workshop compliments and *A*s at face value. They still went home and revised and revised and revised. Sometimes they even threw out the section that got the praise because they realized, as they wrote more, that it was a tangent—perhaps an inspired one, but a tangent nonetheless. Even my published novelist friend who pleaded the importance of drafting in "Drafting" also admitted that he does significant work in revision and that he's even "spent years of hard work rewriting [his] latest project." The importance of the draft hardly negates the crucial nature of revision.

I have a theory, too, for why so many writers *do* get *A*s on papers they wrote the night before: It's because "a writer" tends to be better with grammar and basic literary analysis than her peers, who don't consider themselves writers and therefore don't sit around thinking about words in their spare time like the writers do. To use an analogy, someone on the swim team is likely to be better at soccer than a nonathlete because his muscles are just in better condition. So in a class where almost everyone is turning in a first draft for a grade, the "writer's" draft is more likely to get the high score. It's not because that draft was a glowing specimen of fine prose and brilliant thinking.

Sorry to break that to you.

Of course, there are times when you just *get it right* in the first draft. I tend to think it happens most when you've been kicking the story around for a long time before you actually start to wrap sentences around the ideas. The great news is that the more you write, the more you practice your craft, the more times your draft *will* have great moments that need no changing. My drafts now are far less embarrassing than my drafts from high school, or even from my MFA years a decade after high school, because all those years of hearing feedback and practicing revision alerted me to specific weaknesses I see all the time in my drafts, that I'm now on the alert to avoid.

Show, don't tell!

Got that? Yeah, finally.

WATCH YOUR
Soap Operas

*A*ll through middle school and high school, my afternoons were marked by a special hour spent with my mom, during which we would hunker down on the couch and watch *Another World* (*AW*). Yes, a soap opera—one of those long-running (thirty-five years for *AW*, starting in 1964!) television dramas that keep millions of viewers in their thrall for big chunks of their adult lives.

Like many women, my mom got hooked on *Another World* when my brother and I were tots and she needed an escape in the afternoon, an hour of her time that would entertain and refresh and wouldn't take too much energy. I didn't start watching it myself until the summer after sixth grade (this is a rough estimate since I don't quite remember when I started watching regularly, and I also suspect that my mother wouldn't have let me watch such a lurid program until I was a little older), but I have distinct memories of glimpsing it on my parents' bedroom television in the afternoon when I was a child, and of hearing my mother discuss the fates of particular characters with her friends by the sides of various pools in the summer and in the kitchen in the winter. Would Jake cheat on Marley with Vicky?

Would Carl Hutchins come back from the dead? Whose daughter was Lorna, really?

I vividly remember the summer afternoons I spent watching *Another World* with my mother, maybe because, free of school and extracurricular activities, we could actually watch it live. It was on at one in the afternoon, and we would often wait to eat lunch on the couch as we watched. Before the show started we would make sandwiches in the kitchen and guess what was going to happen in today's episode, ratcheting up our excitement with every uttered hypothesis, every slice of mustarded bread. For me, this was the very definition of the lazy summer afternoon, spent eating something delicious and immersing myself in, well, another world.

During the school year, when I was a student and my mom a teacher, she taped the show so we could watch it later in the day. Usually, we turned it on around four, after I had finished some homework or had come home from a club meeting, and before Mom started getting dinner ready. As we watched on the couch, snuggled under blankets, the sun would set outside, the darkness slowly cocooning us in with our beloved characters. My dad, who'd long made fun of us for our obsession, even started watching the show with us during the years when Anne Heche played good twin Marley and evil twin Victoria—then, we'd wait to watch the show until after dinner when he could watch it with us. Few weeks went by when we wouldn't rib him for succumbing to the pleasures of the soap opera. His defense, that Anne Heche was a superlative actress, would turn out to be a good one, as Anne has deservedly gone on to have quite a career on big and small screens.

Now, there are a lot of people who will tell you that such low-brow entertainment is not fit for anyone's consumption, let alone that of an aspiring writer.

They are so wrong. Let me throw down the gauntlet here: I learned as much about storytelling from *Another World* as I have from most of the novels I've read.

This is partly because *Another World* started working on me early, before I really understood what it meant to be a writer, long before it even dawned on me that there were actually writers scripting the show in offices in New York, and that the characters weren't, like, *real people* from literally another world, striding onto my television screen every day and letting me glimpse the most fevered, intimate moments of their lives.

Let me highlight here some of the things *Another World* taught me about storytelling, in no particular order:

1. Characters are of paramount importance. You have to have characters who intrigue your audience.
2. You *have* an audience. Make them happy. (You are your own first audience! Does your writing make *you* happy?)
3. Back to characters: Sometimes the most compelling character, the one you want to hang out with the most, is the evil twin and not the good twin.
4. A moment of humor in a maudlin hour makes all the difference.
5. Setting is important. Whether you have ripped bods swimming in a shimmering blue pool in August, or two older characters dashing off to Europe in the winter, or your fave heroine in a burning house hoping against hope that her prince will arrive, the point is, make sure your setting is well-drawn and exciting.
6. Everyone loves a wedding. Or a murder. Or a person coming back from the dead. Or (fill in the blank with similar big events).
7. Sharing a great story is as good as—maybe better than— savoring it yourself. Writers should want their audience to *talk* about their work.
8. It's great to hang out with a favorite character every day, and even better when they go away for a while, leaving you wanting more.
9. Pacing is everything. Make your audience wait for it. But not too long, or they will lose interest.
10. Watching a character suffer is infinitely more interesting than watching her hang out in the sunset into which she sailed.
11. Be controversial.

You'll note that there is nothing on this list about the finer aspects of the *art* of writing—nothing about the prose or the Big Ideas. You're right. Those things I learned from novels. But none of that lessens what I *did* learn from *Another World*.

Watching *AW* might have been what made me want to be a writer in the first place. I wanted to write something that was as transporting as that show was for me. Also, the flamboyant, boa-wearing novelist Felicia Gallant was one of my favorite characters. In addition to swanning around in over-the-top outfits and giving great parties, she would sit herself down in front of a typewriter and pound out the best-selling romance novels that clearly paid for her boas and parties. Plus her best friend was handsome playboy Cass Winthrop, another of my favorite characters for his dark good looks and seemingly mature, sardonic take on the world (there wasn't much urbane irony where I grew up, so I took it where I could find it).

Speaking of irony, by the time I'd stopped watching *AW* regularly, I actually had a brush with writing for soaps. I'll spare you the details because it never worked out, but let's just say that in the process I glimpsed just how *hard* it is to write for one. There are multiple tiers and teams of writers (and this works basically the same for many television shows): The smallest, presumably highest-paid umbrella group comes up with the long-term story arcs. They then give their story outline to the next group who figure out what's going to happen with each character on a weekly, then daily, basis. And they, finally, hand that info down to the dialogue writers who put the words into the characters' mouths. Whew! Who knew writing could be such a team effort? (Well, it turns out that *most* writing is a team effort—see "Published Writing is a Team Effort.")

And all this writing is coming to a television near you *every day*. *Daily publication!* A dream to some writers, a nightmare to others. I mean, can you imagine being brilliant every day? I can't; in fact, I think I'm late for my nap.

Anyway, the point of all this is *not* that you should find a soap opera and watch it. The point is that you should find a method of storytelling that you love that is *not* reading, and study it. Ask yourself what makes it tick, and why you like it. Let it teach you, and find ways to apply its lessons to your writing. YARN's very own Lourdes Keochgerien made a point along similar lines in her great blog, "Film

= Writing School," in which she discusses several films that have taught her things about writing that no book ever could have.

Television is, of course, a great place to turn these days for lessons in storytelling and character development. *Lost, Glee, Mad Men, The Sopranos,* and *Breaking Bad,* to name just a few, are fantastic examples of the form and have even taken the place of my daily soap (plus, *AW* was cancelled back in 1999, gone the way of so many soaps in these days of cable TV and the Internet).

But watching much-lauded prime-time shows instead of a soap opera won't teach you this very important lesson, which has nothing to do with storytelling but everything to do with being a writer: how to defend your tastes. So many people, including my dad, frowned on my watching a daily soap because soaps have always been considered housewife fare.

First of all, who ever said housewives have bad taste? Hey, it's housewives who keep novels in print, so don't slag them off.

Plus, these terms like "housewife fare" and "geek lit" give perfectly respectable genres a bad rap. Love science fiction? Write it! There are great reads to be written in every genre. Can you believe that some people still consider YA to be the soda pop of the literary world? So wrong! Go ahead and name ten writers who prove them wrong.

So yeah, sure, soaps are full of lurid, ridiculously unrealistic plots. They objectify hunky men, glorify violence, and condone adultery. But they also pull off the miraculous feat of keeping their audience coming back every day for decades.

If you're going to be a writer, it's good to practice defending yourself to the critics of the world, because it's true that everyone's a critic—just wait 'til you get brave enough to show your writing to people! It was easier to defend *AW* than to defend my own writing; it still is, in many ways, since defending my writing sometimes feels like defending myself. I'm just glad I got the practice before the critiques got personal.

And if someone tries to tell you to change your tastes, ask them for *their* ratings.

MY FIRST *Big* MISTAKE

When I was a junior in high school, I made my first real mistake as a writer, and by "real," I mean a mistake with consequences. I was the assistant editor of the St. Mary's High School *Kettle*, a position I'd worked hard to attain since I was a freshman. Before I came on the scene, there had been no official place on the newspaper's masthead for first-year students; sure, I could have groveled to the upperclassmen editors for an article assignment or two, but there was no way to be on the staff and part of the club. This angered and concerned me at the same time: How was I supposed to distinguish myself from the throngs of other freshmen (whom I incorrectly assumed *all* wanted to compete with me for a space on the paper's staff)? How could I make it clear that I was *special*?

I understood that I was a *freshman*. And it was only September. Despite my unwarranted sense of specialness, I was also full of a sense of my smallness in the big, intimidating world of high school. To intensify the stress, St. Mary's was a brand-new environment with new people for me. I had transferred from a public school to a private one, so none of the eighth graders I'd known as a seventh grader were sophomores who could now defend and help me. I felt pretty darn alone and small.

With all these competing emotions coursing through me—my specialness, my intimidation, my sense of injustice against freshmen—I huffed into my seat at the dinner table one night and my parents coaxed out of me that the reason I was sulking was this problem with the newspaper.

My dad responded with something like, "You're not going to let that stop you, are you?"

I almost certainly rolled my eyes in a dramatic fashion and said with *du-uh* in my voice, "I guess I have to."

But my dad was not about to let it go. "Kerri, that attitude will get you nowhere," he said. Then he told me a story about a guy in his high school—Joe, maybe—who had been the first freshman in the history of the school to make it onto the varsity football team (my dad was the center) because Joe had showed up half an hour before practice started on a Saturday, brought the coach a cake his mom had made, and showed him how fast he could run and how far he could throw a ball. My dad has always been full of stories like that.

I am sure that in reply I played dense on purpose, because I was simultaneously relieved and irritated that he was going to have an answer for me. So I said, "You want me to bake a cake for the faculty advisor of the newspaper?"

At this point, of course, my dad knew he had me, so he didn't get annoyed with my cheekiness. He just laughed and said, "Well, cake always helps. But I meant that you should find a way to show him you're special."

"But *how*?" I whined.

This time my mom, thinking like the teacher she is, chimed in, "Is there something you could do for the paper that they don't already do?"

I thought about this for a minute, and then replied that I didn't know.

But I understood what they were getting at.

I'm not sure who—me or my parents—came up with the idea in the end, but it worked. There was no music and movie review column in the newspaper! I loved movies! Plus, I played flute and piano, so I knew a thing or two about music. I was going to be the Arts editor for the *Kettle*!

Guess what? It worked.

After outlining the idea and writing a sample review, I screwed my courage to the sticking place and pitched the idea to the faculty advisor for the paper. He ran it by the editorial team for that academic year, and they said yes.

As an aside, I'm proud to say that the column remained a place for promising freshmen writers through my years—and then my younger brother's years—at the school. A quick look online shows me that although it's now called "Art/Poetry editor," the position is still there, and I hope it's occupied by a hungry young freshman.

All of which is a very long-winded way of explaining why the newspaper meant so much to me. By the time I was a junior, even though I wasn't yet editor-in-chief (and it was a foregone conclusion that I would be the following year), I felt like the paper was *mine* on some level. Since I was a freshman, I had helped shape and change the paper, and I was extremely proud of it.

Okay, so there I was, an upperclassman editor of the paper, when the faculty advisor, who was also now one of my favorite teachers, pulled me aside one day and asked if I would be interested in writing about something for the paper.

Full of a sense of my importance—here was a teacher asking *me* to do something for him, for the school!—I listened carefully to his pitch.

It was about school vouchers in California. Basically, the school, being a private institution, was excited about vouchers, and it truly believed that vouchers would make it possible for a more diverse group of students to attend the school. I won't get into the politics of school vouchers here, because that's really not the point. The point is that I was being asked to write something for the school paper, and I could tell what the school thought about the issue.

No one asked me to write for or against vouchers. My teacher—who believed scrupulously in American rights and freedoms and in encouraging independent thinking in his students, who had supported me one-hundred percent when I wrote a scathing critique of the war in Kuwait that temporarily lost me a few friends—even suggested that if I felt more comfortable, I could write a straight news piece about the issue and not an editorial.

Still, I walked away from that meeting feeling uneasy. I was what you'd call a "good girl." I got straight As and I actually liked my teachers—and wanted my teachers to like me. I was a people pleaser. I could tell which opinion on vouchers would please the most people at the school. And at the time, I didn't have strong opinions on this particular subject, so who cared what I wrote?

I read some pamphlets about vouchers, as this was before the days when I could Google the subject, and talked to my parents about the issue, both about school vouchers as a controversy, and about what I should write. Because they are my parents, they simply told me to write what I thought was right.

The problem was there were many versions of "right" in this situation. One "right" was ingratiating myself with people. Another "right" was digging deeper into the topic and doing some soul-searching to decide what I really thought, then writing that opinion. Yet another "right" was telling my teacher that I didn't feel comfortable writing about vouchers at all and asking one of the younger, more political editors to tackle the subject.

In retrospect, I realize that I could have written anything I wanted and none of my favorite teachers would have thought any less of me; they certainly hadn't thought less of me for the Kuwait piece, and I'm sure that many of them supported the war and thought I was woefully mistaken. Even at the time, I suspected I could have written my own truth about vouchers. But I was confused: Didn't being a good student mean doing what you knew your teachers and school *most* wanted you to do?

I'm also an inveterate worrier. So I worried about this a lot. I worried before I wrote. I worried while I wrote. I worried after I turned in the opinion piece that I knew my heart wasn't adequately in.

I worried a little less when I got compliments in the hallways from favorite teachers, telling me that they liked what I wrote and what a great issue of the *Kettle* it had been overall.

I started worrying again, though, when my best friend, someone two years younger but much more acutely liberal and political than I was, asked me, "Is this really what you think?"

"Yes," I said, before changing the subject.

Because I knew. I knew I hadn't done enough research to properly educate myself about vouchers, because somehow I knew—I *knew*—that if I had, I'd have been persuaded to write against them. Even then I knew I was a blue dot in a mostly red sea, and I knew that being pro-voucher was being red.

I have always been ashamed of having done this, of letting my need to be liked overshadow my innate writer's need to write what I truly believed.

Eventually, the hot-hot-hot shame died down. But the embers still glow in the back of my mind, and they flame up again every time I think about writing what will please instead of what is right.

In fact, I'm feeling a little hot right now. It's not easy to confess this to you.

Given my long-term shame over this seemingly small thing that happened (*gulp!*) more than twenty years ago, you'd think that I would never make the same mistake again, because its lesson had been so branded into my psyche.

You'd think that, but you'd be wrong.

I have made different versions of this mistake again. Never in a way that shamed me—no, I'm proud to say that I never again wrote against what I believed. But I *did* write things that others thought I should write. I *have* allowed myself to be convinced to write things I hadn't intended to write.

Take the mystery novel, for instance. I never intended to write one. I had never even read one. Well, I had read a "literary mystery" here and there, but I was not what anyone would call a mystery buff, one of those awesome readers who keeps the publishing industry afloat by buying and devouring paperback after paperback.

Back when we were first dating, Mike convinced me to watch Britsteries on PBS (in case you're not up on your public television lingo, that's British + mystery = Britstery), when I was at a bit of a crossroads writing-wise. I'd just finished my MFA thesis, which consisted of a novella and short stories, all of which I was having trouble getting published in literary journals. Mike and I used to chat about what I should write next that would 1) be fun, and 2) actually sell. At some point he suggested I write a mystery. After all, I was having fun watching them on PBS.

I liked the idea at the time. In fact, I loved it. A week before his suggestion, I'd had no thought of writing a mystery, so I was shocked to discover how quickly a main character and a storyline developed in my mind. Julia Blackwell was my character's name, and she was ripe for a series of mysteries, I humbly thought: A recently widowed English professor, she would solve each case based on their parallels to a particular piece of literature. I'd start with *The Great Gatsby*, one of my personal favorites.

I launched in with gusto. I started reading mystery novels of various types to study how they were crafted, and Mike and I upped our intake of Britsteries. I started typing away and felt immediately comfortable with Julia and her plight. Ultimately, though, I had to scrap the whole first draft of this novel, a novel I'd drafted diligently for six months, then revised for another three months. When I gave the manuscript to some close writer-friend-readers, I got similar feedback: The characters were great, but the plot wasn't working.

Okay, fine. I'd suspected that. I was learning to write a mystery. Could I really be expected to get it right on the first try? I was going to cut myself a break.

I took a deep breath and started over, with the same heroine, same *Gatsby* parallels, but otherwise a very different story with a different cast of characters.

This is the novel that got me my agent.

So why is it in a chapter with "mistake" in the title?

Because not all mistakes are bad.

Not all mistakes are even wholly mistakes. The mistake here was in my first draft—I tried to write a book, a standard mystery, that wasn't "me." I knew this even as I tied myself into a mental pretzel trying to plot out that mystery, but I was determined to try. But the book didn't work.

That was a mistake.

The second, then third and fourth, drafts were not mistakes, even though the novel that resulted was not a standard mystery. While my agent loved it—and I was very happy with it—the editors we sent it to couldn't figure out what it was. It wasn't mainstream mystery enough, but it wasn't quite literary enough to be a stand-alone novel, either.

Was that also a mistake?

I don't think so, and not just because I got an agent out of it.

Writing all those drafts taught me as much about writing as watching soap operas—well, almost! Even trying out what I perceived to be the mystery formula taught me the benefits of pacing and careful outlining, two elements of writing craft I hadn't given much credence to before. Scrapping that first draft taught me, among other things, resilience, and how to write a mature, fully formed novel. I'd abandoned my first and second finished novels when the going got tough, when the plot and characters and feedback all got to be too much for me to wrap my head around (a different kind of mistake). I wasn't going to let that happen again, and I didn't.

That was definitely not a mistake.

COME AT IT FROM *the Side*

*I*n Scott Westerfeld's edgy vampire novel *Last Days*, teen musician Pearl is always using the word "lateral" to describe ideas and music she likes, as in: "*What am I listening to? Oh, just this lateral new band.*" She means that surprising, cool art is often created when the artist comes at it *from the side*, as opposed to head-on. People expect you to think about your work from the front, head-on. This approach works great for school essays, in which you answer a question or prompt using facts to back up your argument. For your creative writing, though, I find that it works much better to go lateral and come at it from the side, because that is the approach that will produce the most surprising, page-turning results.

I'm going to be completely *un*lateral here and get into a few straight-up examples of laterality in recent novels I've admired, and then I'll get back to how all of this applies to us on the long road of the writing life. Yes, this chapter contains spoilers. Just a few, but I promise that the books I'm discussing are so rich and complex, they are worth reading even if you do glean bits of their endings from what I have to say about them.

There are plenty of ways to approach your writing from the side, and for plot, there are few better examples than Libba

Bray's *Going Bovine*, which won the 2010 Michael L. Printz Award from the American Library Association. Did she just look up from her coffee one morning and say, "I'm going to craft a truly ambitious work of literary YA about, of all things, a pot-smoking loser named Cameron who gets mad cow disease at sixteen years old."? Not only that, but she masterfully, magically coaxes us into loving Cameron and all his issues by the bittersweet end of the book.

Okay, lateral: mad cow disease! Then there is Gonzo, the morbid and hilarious dwarf, and the garden gnome who actually talks and thinks he is the Viking god Balder, *plus* an angel named Dulcie, and a road trip to end all road trips. And I haven't even gotten into what all these wacky characters actually *do* in the 480 pages that absolutely *fly* by. It may all be patterned on *Don Quixote*, but that doesn't lessen its laterality—in many ways, the parallels intensify it.

I don't know Libba Bray personally, though I hope to meet her one day if only so I can ask for her autograph, and I'm glad I don't know her for the purposes of this chapter, because if I did, it would be way too easy to just call her up and ask her how she came up with this stuff, to ask her for her secret to lateral thinking. The truth is that authors don't always understand the mysteries of their own greatest works anyway. As Milan Kundera wisely put it in his erudite but also practical and useful *The Art of the Novel*, "Not only is the novelist nobody's spokesman, but I would go so far as to say he is not even the spokesman for his own ideas ... great novels are always a little more intelligent than their authors."

Going Bovine is so full of lateral thinking that the only possible way I can conceive for it to exist is that Libba Bray just let her imagination run wild.

That is much, much harder to do than it sounds.

Generations of writers (the Beats of the '50s) and painters (Surrealists) actually felt that they had to take drugs to get their imaginations primed for higher-level imaginative thought. In these post-Harry Potter days, though, we now know that no writer needs drugs to get their imaginations moving in a sideways direction.

Not that all of us should be striving to write on the edge like Bray, all the time. No, that would be exhausting. I do think, however, that when we sit down to write, we should feel ourselves capable of it. I wish I had advice for how to get into the right head space for extreme lateral thinking. As with all thinking in writing, though, there is no formula. I can tell you with certainty that part of what would keep *me* from writing a book like *Going Bovine* would be self-censorship, that evil little voice inside my head that says, "That's stupid," or, "Only you care about that." *Mad cow disease*? The evil voice would say, "How 1997."

I would have to muzzle that voice in order to think as laterally as Bray.

What an empowering thought.

I'm going to need a lion-sized muzzle.

Sometimes coming at it from the side is a quieter, more academic enterprise, as in the books of Jennifer Donnelly, who wrote the YA novels *A Northern Light*, a Printz Honor Book, and *Revolution*, as well as a few historical novels technically for adults. *Revolution* in particular is a lushly detailed, double-barreled story (half in contemporary Paris and New York, half in eighteenth-century Paris) about a musically gifted teen girl who stumbles on a wormhole in Paris that transports her back more than two hundred years. Oh yeah, and it's also about the lost heart of a French king, fireworks exploding over a city at war, and a girl falling in love for the first time, among other things. It is brilliantly lateral in its treatment of history, geography, and the human heart.

With all due respect to Kundera, there are at least a few things that writers can and do know about their writing process. YARN interviewed Donnelly and she shed some light on the origins of her novels: "Something grabs me and won't let go," she told us. "In *Revolution*, it was an article in *The New York Times* that showed a tiny dried heart in a glass urn. These things stir up really strong emotion in me, and I have to deal with that emotion the only way I know how—by writing a story." It's almost as if Donnelly took that image of a little heart in an urn and ran at it with her words, *from the side*, taking it completely by surprise.

I'm better at analyzing plot and character than I am at analyzing language, which is a good thing, since if I was better with language, this chapter would be going on and on with more examples of laterality. Just consider the novels-in-verse of Samantha Schutz, Terra Elan McVoy, and Sonya Sones. I mean, a whole novel written in poetry. Talk about taking a form (the novel) and coming at it from the side with your fancy-schmancy language. I could never do that, no matter how freed I allowed my imagination to become.

Even though I'm going to make a stop at the Little Shop of Muzzles in my mind before I sit down to my next novel, I'm still not satisfied that muzzles are the only answer to freeing my imagination.

Here's a different kind of example of lateral writing that might help us further.

One of my favorite assignments to give creative writing classes asks students to address a prompt I pretty much ripped off of David Lodge. In his novel *Thinks...*, one of the characters is a creative writing professor who asks her students to imagine themselves as bats and write a short passage from the point of view of a bat (if you want to know *why* she's thinking about bats, I highly recommend the novel), but in the voice of a well-known writer.

In the novel, David Lodge crafts such hilariously funny student responses to this assignment, using the voices of Irvine Welsh, Martin Amis, and Samuel Beckett, that I was inspired to try something similar in my own classes. In my mind, the assignment was meant to get students thinking about voice and point of view (POV), about how they shape a piece of writing, as well as how voice and POV are different things but also overlap. I thought Lodge's assignment was genius in the way it forced writers to remove their human selves from the writing in order to really isolate the crafts of voice and POV.

Hearing the results of the assignment in my own class revealed so much more than voice and POV to me and my students, however.

Okay, here was my prompt, an homage to Lodge, which I'm reproducing here in case you want to try it:

> Pick a book or story by an author with a strong, recognizable style (you might also call it "voice," as we have in class). Make a photocopy of one or two pages from the voice you're using as your example, and be sure to provide the attribution (i.e., name and title).
>
> Then, pretend you are a dog (I am not kidding). Write a short passage (500–750 words) from the dog's POV, but in the voice of the author you've chosen. This need not be a full-fledged short story; it can be about whatever you like, as long as it's in that voice, and from the POV of the dog.

As was the ritual in this class for short, ungraded assignments like this one, I asked for volunteers to read their work out loud to the class and allow other students to give feedback. Never had I had so many volunteers to read—students were so eager to share their dogs with the class.

And no wonder! These dog pieces were impressively clever spins on the original voices, sometimes genuinely heartbreaking and sometimes side-splittingly funny (just as entertaining as Lodge's own examples, though my students were beginning writers). Hands down, this assignment produced the best, most lateral writing of the semester. I think everyone in class read their work; I had to block out extra time in future classes just to make sure everyone who wanted to read would have a chance.

Why?

I just dashed off an e-mail to two of the students who were in that class, who are now on the staff of YARN, to ask them why. But while I'm waiting for their answers, the Kundera in me thinks I should muse a bit, too.

I suspect it had something to do with the laterality of the assignment, for which I give all credit to Lodge. The assignment itself was ambitious and forced the students out of all comfort zones; they couldn't just fall back on "I" or any other voice they knew too well. They had to leave those personas behind and fully inhabit the poodle/schnauzer/dachshund/retriever of their choosing. *And* they had to embrace the voice of another writer and give that voice to the dog. Ironically, despite the fact that there were so many restrictions placed on their writing, these restrictions put them in a head space where their creativity could flourish uninhibited.

The reply e-mails from my former students confirmed what I just wrote. To that, each of them added that it was hard to take themselves or their writing too seriously when imagining themselves as dogs, and also they couldn't take anything for granted—since the writers were not themselves dogs, they had to really think about what motivated the dogs. At the same time, one of them said, "We are freed of our fears of getting it wrong, and we can set our creativity loose."

Who knew?

So as I implied before about *Going Bovine*, the keys to this whole lateral thinking thing seem to be not taking yourself too seriously and letting go of your fears and self-censorship. Easier said than done. If you can't get there on your own, maybe it's time to give yourself an assignment. A *what if? What if* I was diagnosed with mad cow disease? *What if* I discovered the heart of a dead French king? *What if* I were a dog?

The crazier the question, the more wonderfully crazy the result? Maybe.

The assignment idea is not unlike the "Random Word Challenge" that John Corey Whaley and his friend Randi Anderson gave each other to jump-start their creative processes (which YARN gratefully got our hands on and published). Basically, they gave each other random lists of words from which they had to write poems. Again, with inspiring results, especially when you consider that Whaley is a novelist, a prose guy. You'll have to go to YARN to read more, but it's worth your while, I promise.

In some ways, this book is my assignment to myself. I had been stalled in my writing for a few years. Oh, I had good excuses: moving from Connecticut to Massachusetts, having my first baby, launching YARN. I was feeling the itch to get back to my own writing, though, in the precious few moments I enjoyed when my daughter Elena was asleep and YARN didn't need my attention. I started poking away at a new novel—two new novels, in fact—but my heart wasn't in it.

I had good reasons for that apathy, too—well, okay, one really good reason: I was terrified, staring down the barrel of my fifth novel, terrified that this one, too, would go nowhere.

I needed a confidence builder.

I needed to not beat a dead horse.

I needed to come at my writing from the side.

Then YARN won an Innovations in Reading Prize from the National Book Foundation, and I got to thinking more about myself as an editor, and how my editing felt like an outgrowth of my writing; I had founded YARN because I'd seen a need for such a journal as a writer with a short story that couldn't be published anywhere else.

I was still on the long road of the writing life, and I didn't plan to get off of it any time soon, but I really needed a new and different project to keep me moving forward. A novel just wasn't going to cut it at that moment, even though I was one-hundred percent certain I had not written my last novel.

Plus, I had this crazy idea to write a book about writing.

I spent most of the summer of 2011 thinking along those lines and soul-searching about what I should do. A big part of me felt like I should be pushing myself on the novel, but a bigger part was getting more and more excited about this book about writing, a book I'd never dreamed I would write. I found myself opening a brainstorming document time and again, filling it with ideas for chapters and notes about what would go into those chapters. I researched similar books that were already on the market and discovered that—miracle of miracles—the book I wanted to write didn't yet exist!

Finally, I brought all this up to my husband on a long drive, while our daughter napped in the back seat. Talking about it with him helped me figure out where my heart and creative mind were. Emboldened, I sent an e-mail to my agent asking what she thought, and I got a very encouraging response. Bonus: It turned out all that work

I'd been doing, jotting down notes and such, was the foundation of my book proposal, so in a way I was ahead of the game!

Then, while I was waiting to hear back from publishers after my agent sent out my proposal, I started on a new novel. You know, to keep my mind off things. To remind myself of why I wanted to write *this* book in the first place. The novel wasn't either of the ones I'd halfheartedly attempted months before. This was a fresh idea, for my fresh start.

Coming at writing from the side, through nonfiction, reinspired my fiction. Go figure. And what a relief.

LEAVE YOUR *Ego* AT THE DOOR

"I also have long loved Keats's idea of 'negative capability' and find it tremendously helpful in the creative process and in life in general."

—GIBSON FAY-LEBLANC

"Nobody prepared me for how goddamned much of myself would be in whatever I wrote, and how I had better be comfortable with those parts of myself before I put pen to paper."

—BRADLEY PHILBERT

*W*hen I started writing this book, I e-mailed some writer friends asking them what they wished they had known about the writing life when they were young. Amid all the very helpful responses, the two I've just quoted resonated with me very strongly because they weren't observations I had heard before. On the surface, these two comments on the writing life might not seem related (even if you know Keats's idea of "negative capability," which I'll explain in a moment), just as they didn't seem related to me when I first read the two e-mails. As I pondered my friends' ideas a bit longer, however, I began to see how much they had in common. And though I had never thought about my own writing in those terms before, their ideas were such profound commentaries on the writing life that I started to see how much application they had to my experience of writing this very book.

Gibson is a widely published poet who has published an entire book of his work, and he wrote a wonderful article for *Maine in Print* responding to Keats's idea of "negative capability" and applying it to his work at The Telling Room, a writing center for writers aged six to eighteen. If you're lucky enough to live in or around Portland, Maine, I highly recommend that you check out this mecca for young writers. In this article, he wrote:

> At the Telling Room, we believe in what the poet John Keats called "negative capability." In 1817, Keats wrote in a letter to his two brothers "…several things dovetailed in my mind, and at once it struck me, what quality went to form a Man of Achievement especially in literature and which Shakespeare possessed so enormously—I mean Negative Capability, that is when man is capable of being in uncertainties, Mysteries, doubts without any irritable reaching after fact and reason…."
>
> When we can sit with our doubts, when we can take risks, embrace danger, and overcome the fear that all might be lost, that is when we—as writers, as organizations, as humans—have the most to gain.

Gibson went on to apply this, quite movingly, to one of his students at The Telling Room who, in the eleventh hour before a paper was due, "poured out a stream of prose that filled pages and pages. When he finally put down his pen, we picked up his work and took turns reading. It was the story of how [his] father shot himself."

And here we come to Bradley's quote. Read it again. It's about bravery in the written word, about how you'd better be prepared to lay yourself bare on the page if you want your writing to mean something. No posturing. No BS-ing. No hiding.

Do you think that maybe this kid at Gibson's writing center had to be brave to write what he did?

Yeah, I think so, too.

Do you think that to live the life of a writer, in a constant state of "negative capability"—with all the doubts and risks associated with that life—that you need to be brave?

Go ahead, roar like a lion.

In his already-classic *On Writing*, Stephen King says something similar: "You must not come lightly to the blank page." Being a master of the written word, and therefore of ambiguity and evocative suggestion, King could have meant, and almost certainly did mean, many things by this, but I think one of the things he meant was "Leave your ego at the door," because ego almost always encourages levity.

It is possible to be brave and *not* leave your ego at the door—some writers are like that, and some of them are very successful, but I'm not writing to them, I'm writing to you. What I'm saying is that in order to leave your ego at the door and write what needs to be written, you have to be very, very brave indeed.

It's probably obvious how this applies to memoir-style nonfiction such as this book, which is largely about the writer. It was always obvious to me, too, but only intellectually and abstractly. Then I sat down to write this book, contract in hand, knowing that my words were going to see the light of day, under the harsh glow of the Amazon review pages. After the first flush of excitement and, yes, *ego* wore off—I'm going to be a published writer, damn it!—guess what was left?

Fear.

Ohmygod, peoplearegoingtoreadwhatIhavetosay.

People are going to read it, and judge it, and judge *me*. What have I done?!

I have to beat the fear monster back and muzzle her every time I sit down at this computer to pour my guts out to you. I am existing in a constant state of negative capability about this book: Will my editor like it? Will you like it? Will the reviewers like it? Will anyone even bother to read it? Is it any good? Why am I writing about myself, anyway? What a stupid idea.

And on and on.

I am sure that when the book actually hits the stores, I'll experience another, perhaps more intense, wave of fear.

It's interesting to me that I did not experience this kind of fear earlier in my writing life. Sure, I got nervous when I submitted my writing to workshops and agents and editors, and when I acted out my stories for OPP in speech, and when I wrote my braver essays for the school paper. But nerves are different from fear, and the emotional wherewithal I've needed to summon for this project has been on another scale entirely.

While it's true that I'd never laid my own self bare before, like I am now, and like that brave young man at The Telling Room did, I suspect there is another reason why I hadn't experienced this fear earlier: Until I was actually going to be published on a book scale, I had not checked my ego at the door. I had come too lightly to the blank page. Writing this book and reflecting back on my earlier days, my grand dreams of publication and interviews on *Oprah*, I can see that I was quite hubristic about the whole enterprise of being a writer.

Also, I was mostly writing fiction. It's easy to pretend, with fiction, that you don't have to leave your ego at the door, for two main reasons: 1) you might feel like you're hiding your writer-self behind a character, time period, geography, or whatever, that is obviously not you, and 2) when you're a writer just starting out with fiction, you're not truly writing it for an audience, because you don't have one yet.

These two reasons are strongly related because it's only when you have secured an audience of book-buying strangers that you begin to realize how much of yourself you have unwittingly put into those supposedly "other" characters of yours. Even if you didn't put a single detail from your own life into your fiction, you've put your heart and soul (blood, sweat, tears, and whatever other cliché you want to insert here) into it. *You* are very much on every page of that story.

When you're writing for yourself, or for your relatively small audience of friends, family members, and classmates, you probably *are* being brave with your fiction because you're in a relatively nonthreatening writing environment. At least, I was. I found it easy to be brave when I didn't think anyone was going to read or care what I wrote. Ironic, I know.

One of the bravest acts of my fiction-writing life was to write a romance novel. Until I decided to write one, I was the kind of writer who scoffed at such writing, despite my affection for soap operas. During my first year in graduate school, however, I had a change of heart. I thought, *Maybe it would be nice to make some money with my writing instead of accepting the life of the starving artist.* I proceeded to hole up in my parents' house while subletting my Brooklyn apartment so I could pound out an entire romance novel in a summer—but not before reading, studying, and thoroughly enjoying about a dozen paragons of the form so that I'd know what I was doing. That novel was the most fun I've ever had writing.

But! Hubris reared its ugly head again. I figured a romance novel would be way easier to get published than literary fiction.

Wrong.

Also, fearing my future rep as a writer of literary fiction, I planned to publish this romance and all the ones that would surely follow under a pseudonym. Though I did tell all my friends, including some in grad school, what I was doing, it wasn't an entirely brave move.

I never had to face the fear monster that would have surely reared its ugly head if that novel had gone to print, but it had taken a certain ego-leaving to commit to writing it, to say, *This is worth my while*, especially when I knew I wouldn't be able to submit it as part of my MFA thesis.

Now that I've had this little epiphany, I hope I'll always be able to leave my ego at the door of my office, and only party with her on the occasions when we deserve it. We'll see. As with most things in the writing life, I suspect she will come and go. Periodically, I'll recognize her, and I'll have to ask her to leave again.

Play WITH YOUR Words

hile I was writing this book, I had coffee with Diana Renn, a YA mystery novelist published by YARN who serendipitously lives close enough to me to share an iced beverage on a hot summer morning. We were chatting about this book, and more generally about our writing processes, and I asked her what *she* wished she'd known about writing when she was younger. Her answer inspired this whole chapter.

She said she wished someone had told her to experiment more with her writing. Calling herself a "chiseler" by nature, she said that, left to her own devices, she would chip away at one piece of writing for ages without moving on to anything new, which she feared might have kept her from trying her hand at other genres and writing more works at an earlier age. Of course, once she realized that this was her tendency, she began to expand her repertoire and wound up writing a gripping novel about a manga-loving teen who solves the mystery of a stolen Van Gogh painting in Japan. I doubt she would have written *that* in college!

After a gulp of my latte, I immediately saw and replied that I am the opposite, and perhaps even *too* inclined to leave one work behind for the next. In graduate school, for instance, when

I found that the workshop format wasn't working well to critique the novel I was working on, I abandoned the book and switched to short stories—and when I wrote short stories, I was all over the place, writing from a variety of points of view about a variety of subjects. When I thought I might want to make money with my writing, I wrote a romance novel. At Mike's suggestion, I wrote a mystery novel. Inspired by, yes, *Twilight* and Harry Potter, I got an idea for my own YA paranormal book and wrote that.

You could say I've been around the proverbial writing block. Many times. I am *not* a chiseler, though as you know from the rest of this book, I *am* committed to the craft of writing and rewriting, which requires me to focus on one piece of writing for many months, even years. I have to admit, though, at times I get sick of those long-term pieces of writing and put them away so I can work on other projects to distract me. Yeah, okay, I cheat on my novels with short stories and essays.

It keeps me from getting bored.

But that doesn't necessarily mean that chiselers get bored. I've noticed that my close chiseler friends have an ability to work on that same piece of writing in many ways. They are open to rewriting a novel from the first-person perspective instead of the third; they are open to adding a new character and weaving that character into all four hundred existing pages; they are open to making their novels funnier throughout, or less. While I tend to perform experiments on many different pieces of writing, a chiseler might perform them on just one piece of writing. My approach often results in more total pages and sometimes a facility with a wider range of genres or styles, but the chiseler's approach often results in deeper, more complex single works.

However, the chiselers and I both have a willingness to play with our words—a willingness to alter both the style and the content of a piece in order to make it the best story or poem or essay it can be—which is something I've always tried to instill in my students.

When I taught creative writing workshops to undergrads, I had a few students whose drafts were smooth to read and wonderfully well crafted. They were so good that the writers usually received uniformly glowing remarks from their peers in class, all of which boiled down to, "Don't change a thing." Other students wrote such ambitious—though sometimes messy—drafts that their peers didn't quite know how to critique them, and so they defaulted to admiration, much of which was deserved.

After I, the annoyingly critical teacher, offered my own suggestions, these talented students often turned up during my office hours explaining that they were apprehensive about making changes based on my comments because they didn't want to meddle with their own unique styles and stories. I suspect that many of these students were chiselers—the kinds of students who'd written and revised and obsessed over their drafts before turning them in for workshop—who'd either fallen too much in love with their work or become too rigid in their techniques.

My response was always, "But is your approach the *only* approach? You can always go back to this draft, so what's the harm in trying something different? Think of it as *playing* with your words." This usually loosened them up. They didn't have to commit to the new version, but they at least had to experiment with a different approach.

The mother-hen teacher in me hates seeing writers, especially the really ambitious ones, unwilling to experiment with unfamiliar styles. It's only through experimenting that a writer can truly find his voice and the stories he's meant to write. How else would my former student have discovered that he could be as good with Mickey Spillane-esque crime fiction as with Virginia Woolf-esque interior drama?

My commitment to encouraging "play" stems from how much I learned from my own experiments. Writing a romance novel taught me about plot and pacing, writing a mystery taught me about the intersections of character and story, and writing short fiction taught me about economy. While I was writing in each of those different genres, I was committed to the idea of publishing each one, but none of them are now in print; instead, they amounted to a messy, wide-ranging education in how to write fiction. I am so grateful for it.

There is also something to be said for not getting pigeonholed too soon. Believe me, there is plenty of time to get pigeonholed later. Publishing is full of stories about established writers who couldn't get this or that book published because it was too great a departure from the kinds of work they had been doing for years—they had, in effect, written their works too well and too narrowly. The only way I can see to guard against this danger is to start out as a nimble writer, prepared to surprise and delight and masterfully mix styles, genres, or voices in a single work, or from one work to the next.

This takes practice and many failed attempts. Actually, let's not say "failed attempts," since that's such a depressing term, suggesting that the attempt was meaningless, when in fact every single piece of writing you produce is making you a better writer, no matter what happens to it. Let's instead say "apprenticeships." "Experiments." "*Play.*"

PART 2

The WRITING LIFE

ADVICE

*W*hen you start defining yourself as a writer, everyone you know is going to start offering you advice, probably because everyone thinks they can write. Hey, they write e-mails and texts and history papers and lab reports and letters to the editor. And they read, too! They read novels and memoirs and celebrity biographies and *People* magazine and your texts and e-mails. They think they understand writing.

Yeah, right. Like they know what it's like to stare at a blank computer screen and feel as if their entire sense of self-worth, or at least their mood for the day, will be determined by the next sentence. Like they know how it feels to study the *craft* of writing with every book they read and every poem they scrutinize.

Most of the people giving you advice won't understand the difference between you and them. And that's fine for this reason at least: They care enough about you and your writing to give you advice at all. Do you know how many people don't give two hoots about reading and writing these days? You probably do know, because you go to school with them. They're the ones whose eyes glaze over when you tell them you love to read in your spare time, or who laugh when you tell them you just finished writing a short story. So, suffice it to say, take your attention where you can get it.

I previewed some of the gems people will bestow on you in my introduction, but aside from all that advice about writing being really harsh and poverty-inducing, I have received one piece of excellent advice that has stuck with me for a very long time. I received it in college, and I'm giving it to you now because I think it might help you shape your own identity as a writer, as it did for me. Like most advice, you're not meant to take it literally; rather, this advice, and other good advice you receive in life, is meant to help you think about yourself in a way you wouldn't have considered without it. So here goes.

This first piece of writing advice I ever took seriously came from a history professor my freshman year at Berkeley. This was a Big Name Professor who had enjoyed a long and distinctive career. The man knew what he was talking about. He was also famous for beginning his classes on medieval England with a novel by Virginia Woolf because he liked the way she thought and he wanted his students to be in, let's call it, a Virginia Woolf frame of mind when it came to reading *The Paston Letters*. We read contemporary Nigerian writer Chinua Achebe in a class about Norfolk in the Middle Ages for much the same reason.

At some point in the semester, I let it slip that I also wrote short stories in my spare time and aspired to someday write a novel. This news increased his interest in me, and he started commenting rather loosely on my sentences. I was never more flattered in my entire school career than when he selected one of my short papers to read aloud in front of the class because he thought I'd done something clever: With my own sentences, I had mimicked the style of the work I was writing about. He took the time to do something like this for each student in the class, but he didn't just randomly compliment us—we had to earn it. He regularly challenged us in class, probing our ideas by asking follow-up questions. I never felt smarter than I did in his class, and I remember thinking that the mark of a great teacher is one who makes you feel really smart, maybe smarter than you actually are. That's an extra small piece of advice—when you get to college, find professors who have reputations for making their students feel smart. You'll get the most out of their classes.

I'm getting to his advice, I promise! A semester or two after that class, I attended a lecture he was giving on campus, and I waited in the long line of former students who wanted to say hello to him. When it was my turn, he remembered my name and greeted me warmly in his grandfatherly way. Then he asked me how my writing was going, and I started talking about my English classes. He interrupted me and said he meant my creative writing. I paused, and said something like, "Fine," because at the time, I was really throwing myself into my classes and I wasn't doing much fiction writing.

Then he said it.

He said, "You have to be careful, Kerri. Academic writing will kill your creative writing."

Kill. That's a strong word.

I found out later that once upon a time, he had written fiction himself, but when his academic career took off, he'd stopped. Toward the end of his career, when he was emeritus and all that good stuff, and he no longer needed to publish academic prose, he started poking away at fiction again. I'm glad. I suspect it nourished his soul. But judging from the comment he made to me, I think he felt he'd gotten to the fiction way too late.

This advice, from someone I respected so greatly, really stopped me in my tracks. Even as an undergraduate, I could see how it could be true. I wasn't doing much creative writing because I was so involved with my classes and the papers they required; plus, I actually *liked* writing papers. If *he* couldn't juggle both kinds of writing, how was I possibly going to do it? For one thing, if I did choose an academic career, where would I find the *time* for creative writing? From what I could see, researching and writing as a graduate student and professor could literally go on all day and night, forever, and it still wouldn't all get done. Plus, I was too conscientious to shirk my professional responsibilities for a speculative pursuit like fiction.

He was also talking about something deeper than time; he was talking about the way in which academic writing—with its jargon and footnotes and groundedness in rationality—was antithetical to the kind of imagination good fiction requires. He was saying that the factual way I'd have to think to be an academic would stifle and eventually *kill* my imagination.

Well, I wasn't going to let that happen to me. Thanks goodness I'd gotten this advice so soon!

I started making different choices, like taking a creative writing class and deciding *not* to apply to graduate school for a Ph.D. I tried to do more creative writing in my spare time.

His advice set me on the path to becoming a writer. A creative writer. Everything else I've done in my professional life—working in a bookstore, managing an olive oil shop, being a personal assistant, getting an MFA, teaching writing, founding YARN—has been part of the goal of nurturing my creative writing. In every professional decision I've made, I've asked myself, "Will this kill my creative writing?" If I thought the answer was no, I was at least willing to give it a try. Sometimes I was wrong, and my creative writing would begin to suffer, and so I would quit and move on to the next thing.

It turned out that my professor wasn't one-hundred percent correct. Academic writing doesn't kill everyone's creative writing. In fact, one of my other favorite professors, a Big Time Art History Professor, has lately been writing and publishing poetry (though again, at a later, more secure stage in his academic career). A solid number of novelists either started out as professors or have continued to be professors: Isaac Asimov, Deborah Harkness, Philippa Gregory, J.R.R. Tolkien, and C.S. Lewis to name a few. Not bad company to keep, really.

But when I heard my professor's words, I knew they were true *for me*. It wouldn't have mattered at the time if I could have named twenty examples of academics who were also novelists, because I knew that *I* would not be able to successfully juggle both, and that I would regret it in exactly the way that my history professor had.

So I'm passing along his advice to you *not* because I don't think you should get your Ph.D. and be a professor *and* a novelist. Rather, I'm passing it along so that you can make decisions in your life that will foster your creative writing. Better that you get this advice early, like I did, so you can dodge the bullets that will come flying at you from every direction, intent on killing your creative writing.

In the next ten years, I would get many other pieces of excellent advice about writing from professional novelists, though most of them had to do with my writing specifically. When those novelists gave advice about the writing life, almost everything they said boiled down to the advice I had gotten from my history professor: *If you want to be a writer, don't do things that will kill your writing.*

Simple to say, very hard to follow.

I feel compelled to add a postscript to this chapter, for all the writers reading this book who have no intention of defining their lives and careers by their creative writing. Yeah, you, Writer (I'm still going to call you Writer because in your heart and soul, that's what you are, regardless of the *type* of writing you are drawn to)—you're the one who sees the poetry in computer programming language, or who is equally drawn to architecture and creative writing. You're the writer who doesn't feel like writing a novel yet, and may never. That's cool. In many ways, I wish I were you. You'll have more options open to you professionally.

To you, I'd modify my professor's advice by dropping the word "creative" and just tell you, "Don't do things that will kill your writing." If academic writing is your art, do it. If practicing medicine and writing fiction together floats your boat (as it did Ethan Canin's), sail away! Just try not to stray too far off your path or, like Dante Alighieri, you'll find yourself in a perilous place:

> Midway along the journey of our life
> I woke to find myself in some dark woods
> for I had wandered off from the straight path
> (translated by Mark Musa).

And soon, like Dante, you'll be standing at the gates of your own writer's hell reading the famous warning, "Abandon all hope, ye who enter here."

That's not a fun place to be. I've been there, though not for long, because I know the key question that never fails to set me on the straight path: *Is this killing my writing?*

If the answer is yes, then it's not worth doing.

THE CREATIVE
Writing MAJOR

One of the best things about going to school is that writing in many forms—history papers, lab reports, and even poetry—becomes your "job" for a few years, even though, paradoxically, *you* are paying someone *else* for the work. But that's one of the beauties of being a student: For a few blissful years, everything you do is untethered from reality, which might be why the magical world of Hogwarts can seem so real and true.

And indeed, college was for me something of a Hogwarts experience. Living away from my parents for the first time (I'd never even been to sleepaway camp), I discovered the joys of dorm living (soft-serve ice cream at every meal! *Star Wars* marathons on Tuesday nights!) and of making decisions about small things (my daily schedule, what I wore) and bigger things (parties, boys) without any supervision. Like Harry, Ron, and Hermione, I am still close friends with one of the first people I met at college, who luckily happened to be my roommate. As with them, I discovered in my own version of Hogwarts just how much school can teach you.

Sure, I'd always been a good student. I'd liked high school all right, but it was hard to completely indulge my love of learning in that social fishbowl. In college, I found people who were more like me, and since the university I attended was so big, my own idiosyncrasies often got lost in the highly diverse crowd. It was also such a relief to know that the grades I received in my required classes mattered a whole lot less than they did in high school (any former students of mine who are reading this are probably gaping with surprise at my nonchalance about blowing off classes I didn't like). And also, my annoyance at having to take those classes was thoroughly blunted by getting to take tons of classes I *wanted* to take.

Which brings me to art history.

Yes, art history.

By my sophomore year, I had stopped pretending I was anything other than a born English major. I'd actually tried hard to be a history major, because I really did love history, especially medieval history (I'm a sucker for damp castles and chivalry), but the siren song of English classes lured me away. What can I say? In the end, I preferred analyzing *The Scarlet Letter* to *The Paston Letters*.

I also loved paintings (looking at them, not making them) and had fostered this love since the third grade, when my teacher rewarded the class for good behavior by reading books with French Impressionist paintings in them and handing out postcards with works from the Met and MoMA as prizes in class contests (I'm also a sucker for glistening, pastel days at the beach, haystacks, and starry nights). Eleven years later, when I had a humanities requirement to fulfill with a discipline other than English, I was idly flipping through the course catalogue and spotted a whole section called "Art History."

My curiosity piqued, I looked at what they had to offer.

Curiouser and curiouser. There was actually a *class* on nineteenth-century French painting! With all the museums I'd been to since third grade, all the coffee-table books I'd skimmed on that very subject, I thought this class would be an easy, breezy *A*.

Boy was I in for a surprise. Let's just say, the first day didn't start with Monet, but with the French Revolution, which I knew embarrassingly little about. The details of what I learned in that class are for another book and another time, but what's germane here is that even though it was a very tough class and I was completely in over my head in a room full of multilingual, world-traveled art history majors, I love-love-loved that class, and I went on to minor in art history.

My study of art history has had a powerful, long-term influence on my writing. I've written about painter characters, art critic characters, gallery assistants, an art thief, a sculptor, and art forgers in Vietnam.* Around the same time I took my first art history class, I also read a novel by A.S. Byatt called *Still Life*, in which she masterfully uses visual imagery, actual paintings, and painterly techniques to weave her story and characters together. I was flabbergasted that combining painting and writing in a piece of literature was possible. I went on to devour many of her other novels and stories, especially the ones in which she uses painting, and to seek out other novelists who employed this technique. Together, A.S. Byatt and art history shaped my writing interests and style for almost two decades.

The very same semester I was taking the nineteenth-century French painting class, I was also taking my first undergrad creative writing workshop, a class I had to audition for by submitting a writing sample the semester before. I remember going trepidatiously to the sunny wall opposite the English department where the results of this audition were posted—*Are you in or are you out?*—and heaving a big sigh of relief when I saw my name among the *in*. I might also have pumped a fist in the air. I was *in*! It was one of those small but significant moments of validation in which I truly felt like I was a *writer*.

I learned three very important lessons in that creative writing class: 1) The feedback you offer your fellow writer-classmates helps you formulate and articulate your own literary tastes, which will guide and shape your writing for years to come; 2) when I implement-

---

*"Trip to Saigon" was published in November 2005 in *Guernica: A Magazine of Art and Politics* (http://www.guernicamag.com/fiction/trip_to_saigon).

ed painting into my writing, people were impressed; and 3) I didn't want to take any more creative writing classes as an undergrad.

That third lesson was a result of comparing how each class—art history and creative writing—was affecting my writing at the time. I decided that art history was having a more significant effect. Unless I went on to get a Ph.D. in art history, which I didn't think I wanted to do, despite my love of the subject, I wasn't going to have the opportunity to take more art history classes again, whereas I *could* get my hands on more creative writing workshops.

Just in case your parents, friends, or other teachers aren't telling you this, I'm going to let you in on an important secret about college: For most of us, college is the *last time* we'll be able to immerse ourselves in subjects we love. So if that's photography, eighteenth-century satire, or chemistry, as it was for Kurt Vonnegut, study it. If it's creative writing ... well, I'm not going to tell you *not* to do it, because it's what you love. But I am going to suggest that you double major in something else as well.

Listen, I have an MFA, so I have a whole degree in taking creative writing classes. I know how extremely valuable writing classes are, and I highly recommend taking some when you're an undergrad. Among their many virtues, the classes help young writers focus on the craft and discipline of writing. They spark and foster friendships between writers that can last a lifetime and even help you get published. But while creative writing classes absolutely will improve your writing, they are not going to help you learn about the stuff that will make your writing interesting, as would, say, pre-med classes, to which the fiction of doctors Ethan Canin and Michael Crichton attest.

Creative writing is also not a pre-professional degree in the way that some young writers imagine. With so many students going to college these days in preparation for a specific job, it's easy to assume that the creative writing major is the answer to your prayers, the degree that will set you on the path to becoming a professional writer. I wish it were! But majoring in creative writing is no more likely to set you on the path to becoming a full-time writer than majoring in mechanical engineering—though if you study mechanical engineering, not only are you likely to be able to secure lucrative employment as an engineer after college, you'll also be able to fill the short stories you write in your spare time with fun details about how to build a robot. By the same token, majoring in English doesn't preclude writing about other subjects as well. Michael Pollan has two degrees in English literature, and yet he is best known for his writing about the food industry, which is strongly grounded in science.

I don't want to sound like I'm knocking creative writing as a discipline, so let me come at this from the side with a related example. In my junior year of college, I managed to wangle my way into a year of study at a university in London. It was among the very best years of my life to date, for lots of reasons (eating dark chocolate digestive biscuits, making lifelong friends, clubbing in the West End, and studying across a courtyard from the Courtauld Institute of Art, which is *full* of Impressionist masterpieces). In exchange for these life-altering experiences in the capital of Great Britain, I did have to remain a full-time student. Such a sacrifice.

Half the classes I took were small seminars with twelve students or fewer. In one of them, on existentialist literature, we were discussing Sartre's *The Age of Reason*, which employs one of my favorite phrases in all of literature, describing a character being unable to produce an "appropriate air of grave vacuity" while waiting for a friend in a dance club and trying not to seem bored or lonely. The book takes place in 1938, and the semester before I'd come to London, I'd taken an art history class about three major artists from the first half of the twentieth century—Piet Mondrian, Kazimir Malevich, and Jackson Pollock—and so as the class read and discussed the Sartre novel, I was brimming with comparisons between the literature and art of that time period.

At some point, I voiced one of those comparisons in class.

In response, one of my classmates said, "I'm not sure what that has to do with anything."

Another said, "Who's Mondrian?"

There were similarly blank looks around our seminar table.

The professor rescued me and validated my comparison.

Contrary to how it may appear, this is not an anecdote about how smart I am. No, my classmates would have seen, and no doubt observed long before I did, the same comparison I had, if their system of education encouraged broader undergraduate study. See, in England, you have to specialize down to just three subject areas when you're in high school, which they call "sixth form." And once you get to university, you really hunker down and do the degree you're enrolled in—English, History, French, whatever. On one hand, that sounds like heaven—no math after sophomore year! On the other hand, it means no art history classes if you're an English major, which makes it a lot harder to make comparisons between two historically parallel developments of art like literature and painting.

Also contrary to how it may seem, this is not an opinion piece about English versus American systems of education. Both systems have a great deal to recommend themselves (and just so you don't think that's an empty compliment, I'll be the first to admit that English students of English literature have read far more important written works, far more deeply, than I have with my American degree in the same discipline).

Rather, I offer this example to illustrate a lightbulb moment in my own education, a moment in which I realized how important it was for me as a writer (of English papers *and* of fiction), to know as much about the world as possible. Had I only studied one subject, my writing would have been as narrow as my studies. I suppose I worry that majoring in creative writing creates a similar narrowness in writers.

One of my previous students that I admire most was a marine biology major in college. She is also a gifted writer and visual artist, but she really wants to study the sea. She threw herself into her study of marine life with gusto, all the while writing and editing for the campus literary magazine and balancing other work-life pursuits. She's had impressive fellowships in America and abroad, some that actually required snorkeling as part of the job. (Talk about nice work if you can get it.) But here is the thing: She could get hired in a minute as a science writer for any publication that might be looking because she followed her heart and studied what she loved, and got darned good at it in the process. She might also be the next Barbara King-solver. I wouldn't put it past her.

Many writers would argue that everything I've said in this chapter is academic anyway (bad but necessary pun, sorry), because really, writers ought to be out *living* more than they are studying. Think of Hemingway driving an ambulance in World War I, or hunting in Africa. Or Jon Krakauer hiking through the wilds of Alaska and Argentina. Or Nell Freudenberger backpacking and living all over the world. Or me, even, living in London for a year where, frankly, I did a lot more *living* in England than I did studying—or, years later, putting together almost all the money I had to visit a friend in Vietnam, a financially unwise stunt that did at least result in my first published piece of fiction.

I think you get the point. If you want to be a writer, everyone is going to tell you you're an unrealistic dreamer. In college you can at least study all those other unrealistic dreamers whose ideas forever shaped our world.

FIND YOURSELF AN *Audience*

Remember that image of me in "Drafting," toiling away on dark and stormy nights, pounding out "Run, run, as fast as you can" on my dad's '80s PC with the green cursor? Well, it wasn't just for my own self-esteem that I was piling up those pages.

It was for my audience.

Heck, yeah. I had people *waiting* for those chapters.

If I was feeling particularly cocky about my latest install-ment, I might print *two* copies from my family's dot matrix printer. Then, at first-period band practice the next morning, I would hand the pages to my biggest fan, an eighth-grade flutist named Dale. Truth be told, I was really trying to get those pag-es into the hands of my big crush, an eighth-grade tuba player named John, as soon as possible. Even though Dale was defi-nitely a fan and I was psyched to get her input, she was also BFFs with John. It was no secret that the hero of my story was at least physically based on John. I was a writer back then, yes, but I had not yet learned to be coy.

So the pages started with Dale and inevitably made their way to John, who would coyly *not* talk to me about what he'd read until a couple of days later. Finally, he'd pass me a note between classes and quote a line from the chapter.

Great. My tween crush was that much closer to my grasp. More importantly, I was often completely shocked to find out who else had read those pages. Sometimes they wound their way back to my seventh-grade English class peers, and I'd receive compliments from classmates who otherwise wouldn't have given me the time of day, including boys and mean girls. Sometimes I would receive second-hand feedback from eighth graders I barely knew and who never would have acknowledged me in the halls, but seemed to have been following my story from the first chapter.

I can't tell you how thrilling this was. It was my first taste of what it felt like to be a writer with (almost) strangers reading who (mostly) appreciated my work. Clearly, it made me greedy for more because, well, here I am now, and you're reading this, and I don't know you from Adam.

It feels great to get this kind of attention, and not just for the obvious ego-stroking reasons. Many times over the years, I got feedback I didn't like from my audience. Sometimes, especially back in middle school, I heard people say I was just a stuck-up writer. Even when those comments stung, deep down I knew I was receiving the biggest compliment of all: People were reading my work. And if they weren't reading me, enough of their friends were that they felt like they had to say something nasty to keep up. Plus, I would learn that comments about *me* had nothing to do with my writing. The only comments I needed to entertain were the ones about my characters, prose, plot, and the like; people who commented on *me* ("stuck-up writer") could go take a flying leap.

Middle school was also the first time I realized that an audience didn't have to be made up of only people I knew, my friends who liked me, or my family who had to humor me. My audience could be full of strangers or even semi-enemies: my mom's friends, the boy I was mean to in fifth grade, my best friend from kindergarten, my (who knew?) doppelganger in Holland. Eventually, hopefully, my audience could include thousands of people I'd never meet. This might be more obvious to young writers in these days of the Internet, where you can blog your way to an audience, but in my low-tech dot matrix printer years, this was a revelation. The wonders of technology aside, though, I'm still frequently surprised by who likes my writing.

Fast-forward sixteen years: I was accepted to the Community of Writers at Squaw Valley with a scholarship, based on a short story I submitted. When I arrived, I discovered that the admirer of that story, the reader who was mostly responsible for my getting that scholarship, was a middle-aged man. Now, the story I wrote was about two twenty-something girlfriends in New York and the romance that comes between them. I hardly thought middle-aged men were my target audience. But the man appreciated how I handled the money and class issues that facilitated the demise of the friendship. While I might have hoped, as I wrote the story, that someone completely outside my obvious demographic would read and like it, I was still gobsmacked and grateful that he had.

So. Cool.

Between middle school and Squaw Valley, I learned many other important lessons about audience. In high school, I found a captive audience on the Speech and Debate team. Not only were my teammates my audience, so too were the speechies at other schools who competed against me in Original Prose and Poetry (OPP). The audience of teammates was a lot like Dale and my friends in middle school; for the most part, they were on my side. During an evening speech class they would all hear my new story, read from those dot matrix pages. My hands would shake a bit, but I'd get through it, cheered on by the widening eyes and anticipatory postures of my audience.

It was tougher to deliver the piece in competition, but easier when I knew I had a friend in the audience. My friends from other speech teams were my competition, sure, but we were also each other's greatest advocates. Once a group of us got to know each other, we'd bring new nonspeech writing to other tournaments and read each other's work between rounds of competition, offering feedback and trading ideas. I found it amazing that writers who wrote such different stories from mine—one about a vampire (in the pre-*Twilight* days when Anne Rice's Lestat was the only game in town), another about a raped nun—would enjoy my much less worldly stories about, say, a friendship between a boy and a girl that withstands the merciless teasing of the boy. I also found it amazing when the upperclassmen heroes of OPP would stop me in the halls as we were waiting for our rankings to tell me they really liked my writing.

The feedback from this reciprocal audience was my first real experience with an informal writers' group, and it reinforced how surprising one's audience can be, in the same way you might wake up one morning and think, "Wow, I'm so surprised Joe and I are friends. He likes international espionage movies, which bore me to tears, and I like romantic comedies, which he will only watch if there is nothing else at Redbox."

There is no accounting for taste.

Finding an audience—or multiple audiences, over time—is also extremely fortifying. In a world where reading might seem to be going the way of the dinosaurs, it helps to discover a cohort of people who still read for pleasure. Not only did those audiences encourage me in those early days, they validated this lonely pastime of mine. It was reading my work through their eyes that showed me the possibilities for my written words and the ways they might touch or even change people.

I've had many audiences for my work, and some of them have been reading me for many years—notably, my mother's friends. Okay, stop. I know what you're going to say. They are my mother's *friends*. But seriously. People are *busy*. These women didn't *have* to agree to read more than one novel in the course of the last decade, but a few of them have. And in fact, a few have *asked* to read the novels I haven't wanted to share, and one of those friends is still rooting for the publication of my first completed novel, a book I wrote a looooong time ago. And PS, they haven't been shy about sharing what they really think about these books, either.

Oh yes, audiences will tell you a thing or two about your writing. It never stops! Have you looked at the commentary areas on Amazon lately? *Everyone* wants to tell you how they would have written your book. Finding an audience early will help you balance your desires with their expectations. Just because Aunt Gail really wants Bella to wind up with Jacob does *not* mean you have to move the plot in that direction. The sooner every writer learns that the better. What's amazing is that even though Aunt Gail would have married Bella to the werewolf instead of the vampire, she still likes your book. She wants to read the next one—in fact, she can't wait to read the next one!

If I were a teen writer today, I'd be addicted to Figment, this very cool website where writers can share their works in progress with other writers and readers. What an amazing opportunity to find an audience, complete with strangers in other states and even countries! And what an opportunity to discover other voices, exchange ideas, and see how your work measures up. Figment also has the benefit of anonymity. If someone rips your piece to shreds, you don't have to be Facebook friends or speech competitors with them, or even see them at your mom's bridge group. These readers are the genuine article, much as those peers from my middle school days were—people who are electing to read your work not because they have to but because they *want* to.

Yes, you have to be brave to share your slavishly crafted words with friends and strangers. Writers don't get enough credit for being brave. But consider the payoff.

Go ahead and let yourself be surprised. Indulge in the ego-inflating benefits. It's one of the few perks of being a writer. Just don't get hooked on that aspect, because audiences will also teach you that yes, clichés be damned, everyone *is* a critic. Sometimes they are right, sometimes not. But you'll never know unless you put yourself out there in the first place.

BOSOM *Writing* BUDDIES*

WRITING BUDDY: *A person with whom you exchange writing for the purpose of commenting, editing, commiseration, and cheerleading.*

My first writing buddy was Shannon Marshall, during those halcyon-hell days of high school. Twenty years later, we're still friends, and we founded an award-winning literary journal together. So yes, one of the big reasons to get a writing buddy is the potential for lifelong friendship and professional partnership. But the other reason, more pertinent to this book and your life right now, is the positive effect it will have on your writing and you.

Unlike some of my other writing buddy relationships, the one with Shannon started as a friendship and ultimately included writing buddy sessions. Back in high school, we were speechies together, and while I was swanning around performing my own short stories for OPP, Shannon was busy making a

---

*An earlier version of this chapter appeared as a blog on YARN (http://yareview.net/2011/05/bosom-writing-buddies).

name for herself as one of the most talented female competitors Dramatic Interpretation (DI) had seen in a long while.

My senior year, when Shannon was a hot-stuff sophomore, I was stuck on a story I was writing. The first story I'd written for OPP that year wasn't very good, and I knew it. It was sort of quasi-anti-religious (inspired by some reading I'd been doing about Arthurian legends and early Christianity), and it didn't hang together very well. It was not the follow-up I needed to my junior year winner about the boy who could bring paintings to life. I'd been kicking around another fairy tale of sorts about a girl who encounters a lonely shadow in a forest, but I wasn't entirely sure what that story was about.

Since it's always helped me to talk about problems out loud—be they relationship problems, math problems, or writing problems—I called Shannon one evening and asked if she'd mind being a sounding board. Soon we were bouncing ideas off one another, and the little block that had been damming my writing was dislodged. Thanks to our talk, I discovered what the story was supposed to be about. I quickly got off the phone and started furiously typing away. At other times in the school year, Shannon called me for brainstorming help on a few history papers, and I returned the favor.

Fast-forward fifteen years: After a long silent period in our friendship, we happened to phone each other to catch up and discovered that we were each writing novels and needed feedback. Shannon read a draft of my mystery, and I read a draft of her YA novel. We offered each other comments on the manuscripts and optimistic remarks on the books' potentials and our future *Oprah* interviews.

I can't stress enough the dual roles of the writing buddy: On one hand, your buddy is there to offer totally honest and sometimes difficult-to-deliver feedback (*Have you thought about lobotomizing this part of the book?*). But the yin to that yang is that she also needs to offer the kind of cheerleading every writer needs. When you're a writer, a lot of people are going to be mean to you in various forms: Agents and editors are going to say no and often imply that your writing sucks, peers in creative writing classes are going to tell you point blank that your writing sucks, and your mother/husband/best friend might sometimes think *you* suck for spending so much of your "free" time alone in front of the computer.

Your writing buddy should provide a refuge from all of that. Even if she's telling you that, yes, well, part of your story does suck, she's doing it in a positive, optimistic manner—*Yes, you can do it! I believe in your talent! You are talented! You're a hard worker, and you'll figure out this mess of a book*. This is a different task from that of an editor or any other stranger who reads your work who has no care for your mental health. Hence the term writing *buddy*.

Much to my own surprise, not all friends who are writers qualify for this role. I have some very good friends who support and believe in me and would babysit Elena if I needed extra time to write who are not quite *peppy* enough to be effective writing buddies for me, since I need *a lot* of pep when it comes to my writing. I still give them my writing, and they still read and provide crucial feedback, but they do not fulfill the essential cheerleading part of the writing buddy job requirement. That's okay. I need those readers, too; I just don't have a cutesy label for them.

After Shannon, I had other writing buddies, notably a friend in my college thesis class with whom I shared several dinners as we talked over our papers. After reading each other's drafts, we would sit down with something yummy to eat (I still remember her fettuccini with prosciutto and peas in cream sauce), and we'd comb through the essays page by page, explaining our comments to each other and discussing ways to fix certain problems. I am one-hundred percent certain that the reason I got an *A* on my thesis was my collaboration with this writing buddy—who, by the way, is now an English professor at Kenyon—so I chose her wisely. Recently, as a new mom, I've formed a couple of writer-buddy alliances I can utilize to swap a story or an essay here and there. These relationships have been necessarily short term because of the many other demands on our time (children, work, sleep), and that's okay. Like many friendships, some writing buddies are forever, while others are more transitory. I take them where I can find them, and am deeply grateful when they present themselves.

My gratitude stems from my appreciation for the feedback and the cheerleading for my writing, but also for the affection and friendship I feel for *me*. People are so busy with their own lives that it's really an extraordinary act of friendship to agree to read and comment upon the writing of another person, outside of the requirements of a writing class or formal writing group. My writing buddies have spent their precious time and energy on *me* because they value me and my friendship and my writing, which is exactly why I volunteer to be a writing buddy in return.

Reading each other's work also deepens our friendship. Though neither my nor my friends' work has been autobiographical until now, reading each other's writing has always been an intimate act, a kind of crawling into the other's mind to see how she ticks in her most private moments. Sharing my own work feels a little like sharing a child, which is something I said before I actually had a kid, and it turned out to be completely true now that I *do* have a kid. I feel so nervous about handing over this thing that I love so much, I almost want to snatch it right back. It takes trust to hand it over and believe that my friend is going to treat it with love and respect. When all goes well, we're tighter than ever.

I try to be a good writing buddy in return, to hold up my end of the bargain. When I read, I look for the best, shiniest parts of the draft—zinger phrases and sentences, unique characters, and startling turns of events—and I *always* deliver compliments on those items first. Once I've made my suggestions for improvement, I enter the true cheerleading phase of the conversation and refer back to the best parts again, because I find that writers need the most encouragement at the end of a critique. That's the time for, "This is such a great project. When do you plan to finish it? Can I read it when it's done?" The key is that you have to mean it. You can't be a fake writing buddy. You can only fill the role for someone you like a lot, whose writing you really do admire. Which is another reason why a writing buddy is such a rare gift—you both have to actually *like* each other and each other's stuff.

It's rare, but not impossible. On the long road of the writing life, which every writer essentially travels alone, it really is a gift to find a fellow traveler who can share the burdens and joys for a while. Keep your eyes open, and you'll find one or two along the way.

WORKSHOPS AND *Writers'* GROUPS

*T*ake them! Start your own!

Even though this unadulterated enthusiasm seems to fly in the face of what I said three chapters ago, I have nothing but praise for these kinds of writing circles. Just so we keep our terms straight, I'm going to use *workshop* to refer to formal classes in creative writing. A teacher or leading expert-writer almost always leads a workshop. I won't focus on school-based workshops in this chapter because I just dedicated a whole chapter to creative writing classes. But not all workshops happen in school; some are offered in after-school and summer programs, perhaps in your neighborhood community center or local teen writing center; some can be taken for school credit, and others cannot. Whether they take place in school or outside of it, workshops offer many of the same benefits as *writers' groups*, which are informal but organized groups of writers who meet regularly to discuss each other's writing. In a writers' group there is no teacher.

I've participated in just about every kind of workshop and writers' group as a student, teacher, and peer-contributor.

While writing my first novel after college, I joined a four-person writers' group who met biweekly to critique each other's manuscripts; I attended the Community of Writers at Squaw Valley as a student; I took a creative writing class in college and went on to get my MFA; after graduate school, I taught several independent workshops in my community, some at the library and others through the town's continuing education program; as a professor, I taught a multitude of writing classes, from freshman composition to advanced fiction writing. Each one of these experiences moved my writing forward in important ways—so much so that I wish I'd known these kinds of groups were available to me when I was in high school, because I would have looked harder for them, especially the less formal kinds that you don't have to take for a grade or school credit.

Perhaps more important than the feedback I received on my writing are the friends I made in these workshops and groups (even when I was the teacher). I cannot overstate the importance of friends in the writing life. Had they not read my work, saved me from despair when I was in the trenches of a novel, and picked me up when I was flat on my back with worry and doubt, I may just have stopped writing altogether. Then I would have spent the rest of my life regretting and wondering what could have been—a writing version of all those people who regret having given up the piano when they were young. It's not so much that they wish they were bowing at Carnegie Hall as that they wish they could sit themselves down at a party and play a few tunes with confidence and ease, and feel artistically refreshed and fulfilled as a result. I don't want you to be that regretful person either, even if your goal isn't and never will be Carnegie Hall.

Some of the friends I've made through workshops and writers' groups have been happy surprises as well, people I never would have met otherwise. One is a very successful finance guy who was working on a novel when I started a local writing workshop. At that time, I was the expert in the room, though I was probably fifteen years younger than he was. Today we are more like peers, since he's been writing diligently for the last decade and has been through the publishing wringer just like I have. It's great to catch up with him on the phone or over coffee, and his perspective on writing and publishing is always interesting to me because he's doing it on the margins of his quite successful financial career. I admire his dedication to writing as much as I do those who starve for their craft, and in some ways what he does "costs" him more—not more money, but far more time and energy.

The great thing about participating in a workshop or writers' group outside of school is that it removes any need for teacher pleasing. At your local community or writing center, there may very well *be* a teacher leading the workshop, but that person is not present to evaluate your writing for a grade that goes on your record. Rather, he's there as a kind of resident expert and guide to introduce you to a few techniques and cheer you on as you experiment with new ideas. If you're nervous about your writing, there is no better place to start because, in general, you're in a room with a bunch of other new writers who are equally nervous about their writing.

If you're growing up in a place where there are no brick-and-mortar opportunities offered to young writers, have a look online. Figment, Writer's Digest, Yeah Write, and the Gotham Writers' Workshop are excellent places offering online workshops to young writers, and there are many more. As a bonus, you can be relatively anonymous there, which saves you the trouble of figuring out what sort of caffeinated beverage "a writer" ought to be sipping while chatting about Kafka.

If you're broke and can't afford a class—and we've all been there—the Internet is still your friend. (And you don't have to own your own computer to access it; try the ones at the local public library or your school.) A whole world of exciting online literary opportunities await, day and night. You can use Figment or Yeah Write's free online membership to start posting your own writing for other members to read and comment on, and you can return the favor by reading others' writing and practicing the art of critique. You can participate in National Novel Writing Month (NaNoWriMo) in November. You can go to YARN or another online literary magazine and read, read, read, then get in on the discussion that follows in the comments area (if you're feeling really ambitious, you can even play teacher *and* student and use one of YARN's lesson plans to teach yourself about various aspects of craft). You can go to one of many excellent book review websites like Goodreads and Young Adult Books Central (YABC), read the reviews, and weigh in on those often heated discussions, too. The more you practice articulating your ideas about writing, the more you'll learn about the craft. You'll be teaching yourself to write, which is basically what all writers did in the days before MFA programs and the Internet.

You can also start your own in-person writers' group for free. You'd be amazed at what you can teach yourself, and what you can learn from others. Your local library is a great place to start asking. Go to the YA section and tell the librarian that you're interested in starting or joining a teen writing group. You may discover that one is already meeting there every Tuesday evening! If one isn't already in existence, you're likely to get a big fat smile from the librarian, who should say to you, "What a great idea! How can I help you start one?" If you *don't* get an enthusiastic response of this kind, go back on a different day and ask another librarian, or go through the same shtick with your English teacher, a local bookseller, a friendly counselor at your school, or even your parents.

Having started my very own writing workshop, I have some tips for you to get started. I got paid for leading the workshop I gave, but these pointers will work for you even if you're trying to get a free peer-to-peer group off the ground:

- Get your parents' permission before you get started. Describe what you want to do and get their support, because they may very well be talking to other parents about what you're up to.
- Design a simple but eye-catching poster that you can print in plain old black ink, on colored paper (people are much more likely to notice a yellow or orange paper on a local bulletin board than ho-hum white). The words TEEN WRITERS' GROUP should feature prominently, and you should include

your e-mail address (though probably not your phone number), and offer up your parents' e-mail for concerned parents who want to make sure you're not a child abuser. Include one or two short sentences about yourself and your interest in writing, like "I write for my high school newspaper and yearbook, but my real passion is YA paranormal, and I'm working on a novel in that genre. I'll read anything, though, and will even cop to a penchant for manga."

- Post these posters on all the local bulletin boards in your town. Some places to check out: the library, grocery stores, pizza places, coffee houses, high school bathrooms, community or recreation centers, bookstores, gyms, and YMCAs. Be sure to talk to the managers at each of these places, because in addition to giving permission to put up your poster, they might take an interest in you and help spread the word to their customers. Warning: These bulletin boards tend to be high-theft areas, and they also get cleaned off by employees pretty often, so I suggest that you check your posters at least once or twice a week and be prepared to put up a new one if the old one has disappeared. I've found a combination of scotch tape *and* thumbtacks to be useful.

- Secure a space where you can meet regularly, like every Sunday afternoon at three. This might be your own living room (*Mom, snacks please?*), a local coffee shop, or a private room in your local library (some have them, some don't).

- When you have enough people to make a group—even two or three is a good start!—e-mail everyone and tell them where and when you'll meet for the first time. You might want to float around a few possible dates or times, then agree on the one when most people can attend.

- Since you started this group, you are its informal leader. Be prepared! The group is likely made up of new writers at a variety of stages in their writing, so it'll help to have exercises ready to go that you can all do together. These exercises will serve as icebreakers, but will also put you on equal footing.

Plenty of books on the market offer exercises like these, and you can buy one or check it out from your library. Then, as a group, you can decide which ones to do together. (For a list of books, see the bibliography.)

- At your first meeting, decide together how you want the group to work. Maybe you want to be able to submit pieces of your novel each time, but someone else wants to work from the exercises in the book to get warmed up. That's fine! I encourage you to be flexible and make everyone feel comfortable and want to return. Decide together what format will work for all of you, and keep everyone interested and meeting regularly.
- Decide how often you'll meet. Every week or every other week is a good guide. And keep it up, even if it's hard to keep a regular schedule, or if you only have half a page of new material to share. Having a deadline is an excellent reason to write.

I'll also share a few classic "rules" for workshops and writers' groups that I've found to be not just helpful but crucial to the smooth running of any writing circle. You might want to run these by your group, and even put them in writing.

1. When you critique, lead with the positive. Make sure to list at least three things you admire about each person's draft before moving on to the stuff that needs work.
2. Remember, you're offering suggestions to the writer, not "negative feedback." There is a difference.
3. Along those lines, never preface a suggestion with, "No offense," or, "Maybe this is just me, but ..." because both of those should go without saying, and to say them makes the suggestion sound and feel more like a personal attack than a thoughtful critique on the manuscript, which the writer is at liberty to take or leave.
4. If you're reading a novel, critique with an eye forward; consider what might happen next and what the writer is setting up in those early pages, and remember that novels unfold more slowly than short stories. What do these chapters get you ex-

cited about? What do you want to know more about? What could the author reconsider later after she's written more?

5. Don't bother with nitpicky sentence-level edits for any piece, since you're probably all turning in first drafts that will be revised and proofread later.

6. Don't turn in more than fifteen double-spaced pages each time, otherwise it will be too much to read. Remember, this should be fun, not a drag like your homework.

If you manage to start or participate in a writers' group in high school, you'll be an old pro by the time you get to your creative writing classes in college. Yes, I really do recommend taking at least one creative writing workshop as an undergraduate so you can experience the rigor only a formal class provides. College writing classes are also taught by published writers who know what they are doing and can give you honest and professional feedback on your writing and the writing life. You might even consider taking a workshop outside your own preferred genre. My own agent, for instance, recommends taking a poetry class if you are a prose writer because of the economy and discipline it requires. When my friend Shannon took a required poetry seminar during her MFA, she briefly considered breaking with prose to focus on poetry; you never know what you might fall in love with.

The great thing about any large, formal program, be it a creative writing major, a summer writing conference that lasts a week or so, or a writing center in which you participate regularly, is that it will offer you *more* than just writing classes. The Community of Writers at Squaw Valley was like a mini-MFA, offering daily writing workshops as well as panel discussions with editors and agents, lectures by well-known writers, readings, cocktail hours where we could mix and mingle with the cognoscenti, and private critiques with the stars of the program. *Plus* I made friends. Opportunities to meet and ask questions of editors at literary journals and publishing houses are always excellent learning experiences. Those contacts are a big part of what you're paying for at a program like that.

But you don't have to shell out your hard-earned cash to get all that great advice. Many organizations offer panel discussions and webinars online for free or for a much smaller sum than the amount demanded by a summer program. If you live near a major city or you're already attending college, have a look at the listings in the local paper, and you'll see readings and lectures and discussions happening all the time with authors, editors, and agents. Check out your local library and bookstores, too. These mostly free offerings can supplement your peer writing group very nicely, and you can use them to fashion your very own well-rounded writing program all by yourself.

Lest you think, however, that workshops, writing groups, and programs consist of a bunch of writers sitting around drinking lattes and discussing each other's work with the reverence and respect accorded to, say, James Joyce, let me disabuse you of that fantasy now. Every once in a while, if you participate in enough of them, you *will* bump into a group like that. In fact, the first undergraduate fiction workshop I ever taught felt a bit like that, even though there were a whopping twenty-five very different students in that class—there was one student writing erotica, another who revered the violent writings of Chuck Palahniuk, another who had recently given up a career in insurance sales to get her college degree, one who was basically raising his baby sister, and a Bulgarian future law student who was only taking the class because she'd had me as a teacher before and liked me (the feeling was very mutual). Suffice it to say, that class came together as a harmonious whole when discussing each other's work, without ego or competition. Just a mutual, heartfelt love of writing, support of each other's endeavors, and a collective sense of humor.

But only one class in ten can be like that. In the rest of them, you might encounter inflated egos, teacher favoritism, competition between student-writers, envy, and a certain snobbery about genres like YA or mystery or science fiction. You should not let any of that stop you from taking more writing classes, though. In a typical class of twelve students, only a few writers are going to be like that, and you don't have to be their friends. Often the good eggs in a class wind up bonding outside of class and enjoying the workshop in spite of the rotten eggs. You may even find that the things that get on your nerves will wind up inspiring you to move in a new direction. During my MFA, for instance, my constant diet of literary fiction made me hunger for something different, and so I took time out to write a romance novel. Then a mystery novel. And now I'm editing a YA literary journal.

Funny how stuff like that happens if you leave yourself open to the possibilities.

How Good Am I? OR, THE WORLD IS NOT A MERITOCRACY AFTER ALL

*I*n my early post-college years, I almost broke up with one boyfriend for saying that the quality of my writing would be determined by the marketplace.

Are you kidding? I asked.

Did he not know that many of the most important writers of the twentieth century had made barely a red cent with their work? And that really crappy writing often finds its way onto the lucrative bestseller lists? How could the *sales* of a writer possibly be a determining factor in the *quality* of her work?

This way of thinking, that the best work always rises to the top, is a seductive one. It also works in many realms, like school. If you work hard in school, you're likely to earn good grades and climb to a high academic ranking. If you manage to combine your academic success with sports and other extracurriculars, you're likely to start winning awards, and you'll have a much better shot at the ultimate prize of high school: entrance to an undergraduate institution with scholarship money to boot.

In that way, school is a meritocracy, a place in which hard work and talent merits success and rewards. In America, many people believe that the whole country works this way. If you work hard and turn out a good product, you'll succeed financially and otherwise. Horatio Alger stories of "pull-yourself-up-by-your-bootstraps" success abound. Your history lessons have been full of stories like these. Your own family probably boasts one or two. My very own truck-driver-to-dealership-owner grandfather is an example. I'm not going to get into the politics of this success argument, but I have to present it so that you get the gist of a deeply entrenched attitude that millions of your fellow citizens hold dear to their hearts and will use to judge you and your writing.

You may even use it to judge yourself. If you do, I hope you find success early.

If, like me and most other writers out there, you find yourself toiling away for hours and years and wondering, "I'm *good*. Why am I not finding the success that corresponds to the quality of my work?" I have to let you in on a secret.

The world is not a meritocracy after all.

It is certainly true that there *are* stories—millions of them on grand and small scales—that support the theory that we live in a meritocracy. But millions of other stories demonstrate that we don't, and those get far less press. I could make a list of individuals with stories like this, but it wouldn't be fair to reveal their as-yet lack of success in my book. Just know that I can point to examples in the realms of finance, retail, the law, academia, and the media in which great ideas and hard work have *not* translated into marketplace success.

Try asking your parents about Betamax versus VHS tapes. Betamax tapes were much better products, but guess who won in the marketplace?

None of which is to say that we should give up. This reality does not give us permission to say to ourselves, "There's no point."

No, I'm saying all this to give you some sense of perspective, to help you look at your writing and say, "Just because my writing isn't selling doesn't mean it sucks." In fact, you may very well be the next James Joyce. How should I know?

Instead of measuring your success by its performance in the market, come up with some different benchmarks for success. What kinds of comments have you received from friends and strangers? If you look at your writing from four years ago, can you see improvements? Has your writing earned you something, *anything*, like entrance to a workshop or summer program, a prize in a contest, or a compliment from a teacher? Has your writing pissed anyone off? Has anyone asked you lately what you're working on?

Whatever you do, don't get on the comparison treadmill. If you step on it by thinking, "My writing is better than hers," or, "I'm not quite as good as them yet," or, "I'm way better than he is, and his book is on the bestseller list," you'll be on it for a long time, going exactly where any treadmill takes you: nowhere. Believe me. I know. I've run on it many times and haven't even benefited from the exercise.

The arts are a squishy, subjective line of work, a fact that hit me especially hard one night when I attended a reading given by one of my favorite MFA professors, who has published several novels. That evening, she read a short story she'd never managed to get published, and it was great! Funny and wise and artfully constructed—all the things you want in a short story. Had I been an editor reading it, I'd have published it. Another example: Do an online search for Jackson Pollock and have a good look at one of his splatter paintings. What do you think? Back in the 1940s when he started making them, not everyone thought he was a genius; some people thought he was insane. If you didn't know his paintings were hanging in major museums, would you think they were great, or that your little sister did them? In one of my favorite children's books, a precocious pig named Olivia stands in front of Pollock's *Autumn Rhythm (Number 30)* and says to her mom, "I could do that in about five minutes." When she gets home and tries, she earns herself a time-out.

I think that just about sums it up, don't you? One person's genius is another's time-out.

Before you start getting nervous, let me assure you that I'm the first to admit that I'm not writing unparalleled genius-level "works of art." Most of the writers I love aren't making those either. You don't have to believe that you're breaking uncharted ground with your unrecognized writing in order to feel that it's good enough to commit to continue working on. Every writer has his strengths. For an elite few, that means shaking up the literary establishment with something truly *new*. For most of us, it means something a little closer to earth: Coming up with a unique character, spinning a tight yarn, or writing hilarious dialogue.

For *all* of us, it means continuing to work hard. Though that hard work certainly doesn't guarantee our success, it's equally true that we're not going to get anywhere without it.

Which isn't to say that you should assume everything you are writing is awesome. Not every idea or character or voice or style is equal in quality. Part of your job as a writer is to learn to recognize the difference between good, great, okay, and even bad writing. Some of that process will be highly subjective, and in the end you're the one who has to decide if what you are writing is worthwhile. I tend to think that if there is a voice in your head constantly telling you *boring* or *lame* and then your writing buddy gently breaks it to you that in fact she fell asleep reading your story every night, then it's time to move on. Occasionally, I decide by myself that the writing is bad and I'll leave it alone and abandoned on my hard drive, but usually I need corroboration from a trusted reader.

Conversely, one time I was completely convinced that what I was writing was *fantastic*, and I wrote furiously until I finished, then got *fantastic* comments from trusted readers ... only to discover that someone else had written a novel with the exact same premise and had published it just as I was trying to find an editor for mine. I can't tell you how many comments I got from editors comparing my manuscript to the novel that already sat on the bestseller list, despite the vast differences in the ways each of us handled the material. There was no convincing the editors that there was room in the marketplace for both of our novels. Yeah, the *marketplace*. There's that eleven-letter word again.

Lately it's helped me to expand my definition of what it means to be a good writer or a writer at all. For most of my twenties, I had a little tagline that appeared on my mobile phone every time I turned it on: "Be a writer." For all those years, this meant something very small. It meant, "Sit your butt in that chair and write your novel." For me today, being a writer means writing fiction *and* nonfiction, plus editing YARN and teaching writing. For me, editing and teaching are as much acts of writing as writing itself, because in editing and teaching I'm working with words and literature and ideas and the process that goes into a piece of writing—it's all, in a word, *writing*. To put all this into perspective, Emily Dickinson published fewer than twelve of her more than fifteen hundred poems during her lifetime, but would anyone consider her anything but a *great* writer?

My expanding definition of "writer" has been the product of many years of success, disappointment, and work. I wonder how much frustration I might have been saved if, long ago, I had been given permission to think of other writing-related endeavors as writing—as *good* writing. Probably a fair amount. I hope it'll save you at least a little aggravation.

IT *Should* BE DIFFICULT

"*Anything worth doing is difficult.*"
—COMMON SAYING. ALSO, MARK ZUCKERBERG,
FOUNDER AND CEO OF FACEBOOK*

"*Far and away the best prize that life has to offer is the chance to work hard at work worth doing.*"
—THEODORE ROOSEVELT**

The world is divided into two kinds of writers: those who love writing and those who hate it. But both kinds wouldn't want to do anything else with their lives. I am lucky enough to fall into the first category; my only professional loves

---

*Mark Zuckerberg's exact words were, "Anything worth doing is actually pretty hard and takes a lot of work." Watch the whole speech at http://techcrunch.com/2011/06/09/mark-zuckerberg-to-8th-graders-theres-no-shortcuts/.

**For this and other excellent Roosevelt quotes, see http://www.brainyquote.com/quotes/authors/t/theodore_roosevelt.html.

have been writing related: reading, teaching writing, editing, and sitting down to write. But that doesn't mean it's all been fun, fun, fun, easy-peasy pie.

I have often recited the first quote from the opposite page to my writing classes as they struggled with the difficulties inherent in the process of writing, and I believed every word as I uttered it. As I sit down to really think about it for the purposes of this chapter, however—writing things down in book form is a bigger commitment than saying them out loud every semester—I realize that it's not exactly true.

Cooking, for me at least, is not difficult, nor does it appear to be for Rachael Ray or Mario Batali or [Insert Your Favorite Celebrity Chef Here]. But it's so worth doing.

Kissing. Not difficult, but worth doing.

Driving.

Playing Sunday morning tennis with friends (okay, so playing at Wimbledon is very difficult).

You get my drift. You could name many activities that are not especially difficult but still very much worth doing. It's too easy to wiggle out of the first statement by naming exceptions.

Which is why I have come to prefer Teddy Roosevelt's quote. It contains a kernel of the same sentiment, but instead of martyrishly claiming that *anything* worth doing is difficult, he's saying that you'd be lucky in life to have the opportunity to work hard at something worthwhile. (And for the record, judging from Mark Zuckerberg's entire speech, I get the feeling he'd agree.)

Yes. That is the writing life.

Still, though, I know why teachers and CEOs and other persons of authority get behind the first quote. We're worried that our students or admirers are going to get lazy if we don't instill this belief in them. For the person in a position of power, who cares very much about the future of her underlings, nothing is worse than wasted potential.

In fact, it was laziness that got me into writing in the first place. Everything related to words has come easily to me. First it was handwriting (though I haven't maintained this skill—just ask anyone who's had to decipher my scribbles lately), then grammar, and then English classes. I figured if it came so easily to me, I must be a natural. When I compared my ability and performance in English to geometry or chemistry or, heck, PE, the answer to "What are you going to do with your life?" seemed absurdly obvious. Why would I choose to pursue anything else, like music, which I was also good at, but which I found much, much more difficult to master? Surely wild success in writing was waiting for me around the very next corner.

Unfortunately, that early academic success with words led me down the garden path of overly optimistic thinking. When my first post-college roommate, who was an editorial assistant at a major New York publishing house, read the first draft of my novel and told me that she thought it had a lot of potential and she could totally see it published in a few years, I practically detonated. *"A few years! Seriously?"* I was sure it was going to sell in a few months.

And here I am now, writing this book to save you from disappointments like that—or at least to brace you for the inevitability of those disappointments.

Because even though I did show that early promise, being a writer has not been easy. For me, writing is the "work worth doing" that Teddy Roosevelt talked about, and I am grateful every day that I have the opportunity to work hard at it. And work *hard* I do.

When the going gets tough, I can tell you that it's not laziness that makes writing hard for me. No, I can attribute a much scarier reason to those days when putting words down on the page feels like digging my own grave. Those days when I'd much rather be reading. Or napping. Or baking. Or talking to a friend on the phone. Or being jealous of my friends on Facebook.

I procrastinate. I clean the kitchen. I shop online. I call that friend. I take that nap.

And I do it because something dark and powerful is keeping me from wanting to write that day, even though writing is one of the few professional activities that brings me joy.

Ninety percent of the time, whether I'm aware of it or not, the thing that's keeping me out of this chair is fear.

Fear that what I'm writing is bad or not worthwhile.

Fear that it's all going nowhere.

Fear that what I'm writing is boring, and will surely bore the reader.

The surest way to avoid these fears is to avoid writing. Right?

Sometimes what I'm writing *is* boring or going nowhere. But that's *not* an excuse to stop writing altogether. Instead, I walk away from that piece and work on something else. I get cranky when I realize that what I'm writing isn't "right" for some reason or another, but I get even crankier when I'm not writing at all.

Which brings me to the other ten percent of the time when the thing that's keeping me out of my chair is discouragement.

But if I think more about it, that discouragement stems from fear, too. Fear, again, that what I'm writing is bad, that it will go nowhere.

So that covers the existential reasons why writing is difficult for me. (I hope the rest of this book addresses the remainder of Teddy's quote—the part about why it's still worthwhile.)

There are also practical reasons why writing is difficult.

For one thing, it's hard to find the *time* to write, especially as you get older and the demands of work and home and family and friends increase. I know I gave you all kinds of advice about planners and scheduling in "Drafting," but the truth is that to devote the amount of time necessary to write things worth writing, I've had to give less attention to other pursuits. It's a zero-sum game; there are only twenty-four hours in a day. I had to ask myself what I would give up for writing. Some sleep? The gym? A few coffee dates with friends?

Time turned out to be something of a deal breaker for me, which is why I took a job (teaching) where I made less money than I could have made at a more demanding and lucrative job. At a summer writing camp where I was a teaching assistant, the instructor, who was a high school teacher and published novelist, said that one of the more important questions he'd ever answered for himself was whether time or money was more valuable to him. He discovered that, for him, time was almost always more precious than money. For instance, he'd much rather hire a plumber to fix the sink in order to have the time to ride bikes with his family or work on his novel. I suspect this philosophy strongly influenced his choice of career, since he knew he wanted to write. When I heard him tell this story, I immediately saw my own beliefs in his answer.

It's a question worth asking yourself. It's pretty tough to face your own answer, though, and to know that you're probably going to be sacrificing something you enjoy in order to make your dreams come true, unless you are one of the lucky writers who finds total writerly fulfillment in journalism, editing, advertising, or any number of the other careers that utilize your writing skills on a day-to-day basis. *You*, Lucky Writer, won't have to give up much because you won't be working on a screenplay in your spare time.

Shoot. I said I was done with the existential stuff for this section. Let's get back to practicalities.

It's also difficult to learn to write *well*—well enough to see your name in print. In fact, it's a lifelong journey. I am constantly looking for new approaches to the same old material (since I do subscribe to the belief that there's nothing truly new under the sun), and so I constantly feel like I'm in school, teaching and re-teaching myself how to write a story or an essay. Good thing I like being a student. Sometimes it gets tiring to rarely be able to read a book like a normal person for pure pleasure. I always feel like I need to figure out what makes it tick.

It's difficult to write well but still end up chucking perfectly good words into the recycle bin—or in my case to relegate them to files on my computer that may never get opened—because those words just weren't working, even if I've been writing them for weeks or even months. I once threw out an entire novel draft and started over from scratch, with little remaining but the original main character, because the plot I'd thrown her into was so choppy and disjointed, you could hardly find her in it by the end.

It's especially difficult to write when the stakes are high: when submitting something to a workshop class, or sending it out to agents, or (gulp!) sending it to your editor. Did you know that just about every publishing contract includes a clause that allows the publisher to reject your manuscript if, after writing and/or revising, they decide you haven't upheld your end of the bargain? Those are some high stakes. They make me nervous. But we are in good company: One of my absolutely favorite writers, the winner of a National Book Award, told me once that she'd recently sent her latest manuscript to her editor and she was anxious about the feedback she'd receive. *Wow*, I thought. *It never ends.*

In "Getting Published, Big Time and Small Time" you'll learn that I've been asked five times to revise my work without the promise of publication. Okay. Now let's talk about the number of other flat-out rejections I've received, from literary journals for my stories, and from agents and editors for my novels. Let's just say that altogether, they number in the hundreds. Again, I'm in good company— Jack London was rejected close to six hundred times in his early years***; Kathryn Stockett's *The Help* was rejected sixty times; it took John Corey Whaley four years to find an agent for his multi-award-winning novel *Where Things Come Back*. I'm not sure how many rejection letters Virginia Woolf withstood for her fiction, but the fact is that she self-published her novels through Hogarth Press, which she founded with her husband Leonard. She basically circumvented the rejection process entirely, like so many modern writers these days who choose to self-publish e-books and the like.

I know I talk a lot about rejection throughout this book, but something I don't think I say often enough is how *good* all these rejections are. Seriously. If I had never been rejected, I don't think I'd enjoy my successes nearly as much. Nor do I think I'd be adequately prepared for the critical reception of my work. I have no idea how this book will be received, but I can imagine three possibilities: approval, disapproval, or deafening silence. I've already withstood plenty of disapproval, in the form of rejections, as well as written excoriations of things I've published. Approval would be great, of course, but these days I try to keep my fantasies in check. I'd never thought about the possibility of deafening silence until one of my professors at Columbia

***I found this fact on a very cool website called One Hundred Famous Rejections, which I highly recommend. I also verified the impressive number of rejections with the Jack London State Historic Park.

talked about the reception of his first novel. He said that as he wrote it, he thought with glee of how much it was going to piss some people off, and how much other people were going to love it. And then ... he heard nothing. Few reviews, no mudslinging, no public debate. A deafening silence. Which taught him that not everyone cared about what he wrote. But he continued to write, and now, four novels later, plenty of very important people have weighed in on what he writes.

All of which brings me back to Teddy Roosevelt's quote: "Far and away the best prize that life has to offer is the chance to work hard at work worth doing."

Working hard at anything is indeed difficult. Writing is difficult, and many difficulties will be thrown at us as we strive to do it well.

But how much worse would life be if it didn't offer us that prize, to work hard at our writing? It's something to consider the next time we want to complain about how hard the writing life is.

In Fact, SOMETIMES IT WILL DOWNRIGHT SUCK

By the time I was a senior in high school, I thought of myself as something of a writing stud. Though I still played flute in the band, I'd basically given up practicing, devoting the time I'd once spent on music to words. I was editor-in-chief of the school paper, a position for which I wrote articles and editorials, and I had friends who actually wanted to read my stuff, people who thought of me as "the writer." I aced the classes that required papers. But the main reason for my high opinion of myself was my track record in speech and debate, specifically OPP (Original Prose and Poetry).

What I didn't mention in my speech primer in "Feedback" is that the OPPers were always a motley crew, full of speechies who performed in other categories as well, largely because you could only compete in OPP in the state of California, and you couldn't advance to Nationals in it. In OPP, you'd find suited debaters with a penchant for stand-up comedy, Dramatic Interpreters (DIers) who aspired to write movies, and *artistes* like me who wanted to be novelists when they grew up. As a result, you found every kind of writing in OPP—funny, sad, purple, boring—which was a point of much discussion among my peers and me. How could the judges (mostly parents and locals who volunteered their time on Saturdays) possibly compare a sad tale of abuse or short-lived romance to the hilarious adventures of a talking refrigerator? Humor almost always won the day.

This made my own success with non-funny stories all the more impressive, if I do say so myself. In my three best years, I wrote about a girl who has to choose between a bullied male friend and a love interest, a boy who brings paintings to life, and a shadow that talks to a girl in a forest.

It all started my freshman year, when I placed with the top OPPers in my region, my ticket to the state tournament. This was a big deal. Few freshmen in any category got to State, and I knew I'd booted out some upperclassmen to get where I was going. I did reasonably well at State, but for me that year, it wasn't about how well I did once I was there, it was about just being there—partly because I'd had to convince my parents to let me go at all. They didn't love the idea of little fourteen-year-old me going anywhere where senior boys would be present, let alone *college* boys. But my coach did a great job of convincing them that he'd take good care of me, and I went. What I mainly remember from those spring days was floating around in a state of hoarse-throated euphoria, performing my own story and talking to other OPPers about writing and college and movies.

My sophomore year … I can't remember. How strange. You probably won't remember your sophomore year, either. You're not a freshman anymore, but you're also not a junior or senior. You're sort of nobody. Let's skip ahead. Speech-wise, I know I did well, though better with oratory than with OPP, I think.

My junior year, I was hot stuff. On fire, really. I placed in the top of almost every competition with my story of a boy who brought paintings to life. Every year in each speech category, there is a Force To Be Reckoned With. That year, it was me. I went to State—*of course*. And at State, I went all the way to the semifinal round, where, I would later discover, I almost made it into the finals.

Still. People talked about my writing that year. When I wasn't around, people were saying things like, "Did you hear the one about the boy and the paintings? It's good. Watch out. Hope you don't get in a round with her." Of course, I also had critics, those who didn't like my use of the supernatural or thought my presentation was a bit flat. But whether I was receiving praise or criticism, people were talking. I had an audience.

And okay, I didn't make it to the final round of State that year. But I had one year left. Senior year. The year I was going to get what was coming to me.

I had a bumpy start with a story I knew wasn't as good as the previous one. But then I wrote The Story, a fairy tale about a girl who befriends a shadow in a forest.

You know that tingle you get in your back when you're writing something you *know* is really good?

Yeah, well. I tingled the whole time I wrote that one.

My OPP friends from other schools brushed tears from their eyes when they first heard me perform it.

I had State in the bag. I was The Force.

I'm sure you know what's coming. Want to check the title of this chapter again?

Yeah.

I didn't even place in the finals at State qualifications.

The results were always tacked up on a wall where everyone goes to check them, in varying states of trepidation. I was a little nervous, but nothing like previous years when I'd been less sure of my talent.

Then I read the list.

And I read it again.

My friends looked from me to the list in disbelief.

A hot flush of tears rushed to my eyes.

My coach swooped over and pulled me aside.

"You have to put on a good face for the little ones," he said. "They are going to look to you to be happy for them and also show them how to be gracious."

Yeah, a gracious *loser*.

Suffice it to say, I was not at all concerned about the little ones.

I managed to give the requisite congratulatory hugs and receive the perfunctory condolences and outrage ("The judges were really stupid this year, you wouldn't believe who made it in DI," etc., etc., etc.). And then I broke away and found a sunny spot on the playing fields, and cried.

My first real rejection. A rejection of something I loved, that I believed in and had worked hard for. This was worse than the time I lost a middle school short story competition to a peer who actually used the phrase "like a cheetah about to pounce on its prey" (which I knew even then was hackneyed and cliché), because—wait for it—the judges suspected that I might not have written my own story. Which, of course, I had.

Had I been overconfident in my four years of OPP?

Had I not been sensitive enough to the little ones?

Had I deserved to win?

Probably.

Probably.

Yes.

But. I *had* gone to State as a freshman and a junior. I had been The Force. Those things were still true.

Was I still mad? Hurt? Angry?

Yep.

Did I spend the next several months cursing those judges?

You betcha.

Was I bitter for a long time?

Oh, yeah. (It's almost twenty years later—don't you hear the bitterness?)

Did I hate every moment of clapping for my friends at the awards ceremony later that day?

Hate, hate, hate!

Would I go back and change the outcome if I could?

No way.

This was the moment I learned that writers rarely get what they deserve, a lesson I'm so glad I learned early because it meant that I would be able to put all the rejections and disappointments that laid ahead into perspective.

Do you know how many rejections I've withstood since that day? Hundreds. Rejections from literary journals for stories that I'd written, workshopped, and rewritten multiple times. Rejections from agents and editors for novels I'd spent years writing. The only writing rejection that's ever rivaled that one my senior year was when an editor at a big publishing house met with me in person, asked for a revision of my novel, and then rejected the revision.

Surviving that first huge disappointment braced me. Not only have all the subsequent rejections stung a little less (being rejected is a little like getting dumped in that way—the first time is often the worst), time has shown me that life, and writing, goes on.

I know, I'm starting to sound all goopy and spiritual, and I promised I wasn't going to do that. But I'm not making this up. And remember—I *still* haven't published a novel, so I know what I'm talking about when it comes to rejection. I still suffer from rejection, but I have a little perspective now: Birds still sing, coffee still tastes good, great books and movies still thrill me, and I still have more stories inside me waiting to be told.

The first time it happens to you, go ahead and wallow in it. Eat the ice cream, throw the darts, scream in your room. Nothing I say is going to make it hurt any less. Then, take this book off your shelf, reread this chapter, and pat yourself on the back.

You're a member of the club, Writer. Don't let the haters get you down. Remember how you got into this mess in the first place: Writing is the only thing you can imagine yourself doing.

Go do it.

As Dorothy Parker put it, "Writing well is the best revenge."

But! "YOU ARE RARE AND WONDEROUS!"

*M*y junior year in high school, I came across a copy of SARK's *A Creative Companion*. It's strange to me that I don't remember *how* I first laid hands on this book, since it has had such a lasting impact on me. When I opened it, I fell in love with SARK's colorful, ebullient view of creativity and the world.

Composed of rainbow-bright handwritten love notes to her readers' inner spirits, *A Creative Companion* felt at once dorky and freeing. SARK entreated me to "Be who you truly are, and the money will follow." She made me believe that "Your desire to feel creatively free is very important. The rest is easy." But the most powerful exclamation of all was "You are rare and wonderous!" (And no, "wonderous" is not a typo. SARK is all about wonder *and* wondrousness, so her spelling is very deliberate—though I'm a tad embarrassed to admit how long it took me, a rather poor speller myself, to figure that out!)

This statement struck a bliss-seeking chord deep inside of me. Reading it in SARK's childlike block-print handwriting, I felt like I was receiving a profound message about myself from beyond—not so much from a writer-artist living in San Francisco, but from a life force she was channeling and then radiating through her book. When I read about how SARK's choice to live as an artist made her incredibly happy *and* allowed her to make a living, when I read that the creative life was the *only* life for her, my desire to write suddenly felt legitimate. My goals seemed within my grasp.

Her sentiments and the feelings they inspired were contagious. I brought the book with me to a Saturday speech tournament and read it aloud during the early morning van ride to the school that was hosting the event. By the time we pulled into the parking lot, my friends and I were euphorically screaming, "You are rare and wonderous!" at each other at the tops of our lungs. By the end of the first round of competition, our friends from other schools were doing the same, and we would shout, "You are rare and wonderous!" as we passed each other in the halls.

I'm not sure how I placed at that speech competition, and that's appropriate. SARK and her book aren't about winning; they are about creating and giving yourself permission to live creatively. My friends and I felt unbeatable at that tournament, win or lose, because we were all in this art thing together. We were a fellowship of writers and actors who believed that the power of our words and actions could move people.

It was my *Dead Poets Society* moment. Haven't seen *DPS*? Rent it. Right. Now. I'll try not to drop a spoiler bomb here, but I think it's safe to say that it's a complex movie that's not one-hundred percent happy and doesn't have a cutesy Tiffany-bow ending. But the complexity of the movie wasn't what really did it for me, wasn't what made it a movie I *had* to own and watch many, many times throughout high school and college. What made the movie great for me was the friendship between the boys, a bond forged with the unlikely fire of poetry. In one gorgeous scene, the boys play soccer as the sun sets on a perfectly golden autumn afternoon and Beethoven's "Ode to Joy" accompanies their, well, joy. Joy in finding one another, in finding a teacher who understands them, in finding themselves through poetry.

And note: This is one of my favorite scenes *ever*, even though I don't like sports and I don't write poetry. That scene of fellowship and freedom was the cinematic equivalent of what the SARK-infused speech tournament felt like for me. It's telling that I felt SARK most deeply when I shared her with my friends. I like to think that a writer's desire for an audience is, at its most pure, the feeling I shared with my friends that day. Sure, writers also want an audience for fame and fortune, but I think all those selfish aspirations start with a much more innocent and genuine impulse to say, "Hey, I came up with this super cool thing. You wanna see it?" Sharing our writing builds a community around the things we love, be they vampires, comics, or dead poets.

Those communities can last and last in surprising ways. One of my dearest high school friends, Danielle, went on to collect many of SARK's books, and she's now a visual artist herself. At the end of the school year, people wrote, "You are rare and wonderous!" in my yearbook, and almost twenty years later someone mentioned that very quote when she friended me on Facebook. Two of the friends who shared SARK with me that day are still among my closest friends. One is Danielle, and the other is Shannon Marshall, with whom I founded YARN. All three of us can still recall SARK much more clearly than other details of the tournament or some of our other high school antics. In the years since, the three of us have lived and traveled all over the world, sometimes together and sometimes alone. So far between us, we've had two children and four husbands and written three master's theses, at least five novels, countless short stories, and many editorials for the high school newspaper.

I am still friends with both of them, and I wouldn't trade them for a published novel—and that's saying something. They have supported me and my writing unwaveringly over the years, which is not to say they always just told me I was great. They told me the truth, and I valued and listened to what they had to say.

I'm convinced that SARK, a writer and artist I've never met, brought us closer together that day by giving us a touchstone we'd have for decades to come. If that's not a testament to the power of words, I don't know what is. For me, it was closer to a calling.

PART 3

Looking Ahead:

SUPPORTING YOURSELF, GETTING PUBLISHED, and not GETTING PUBLISHED

IS IT A *Hobby* OR A *Job?*

Writing: Is it a hobby or a job?

This is an argument I've had with my husband Mike many times, and you'll no doubt have it with parents, friends, and teachers as you venture down your own writing path.

Guess which one I think it is?

Yep. Except, I don't get paid.

Which is why Mike says it's a hobby.

See, for him, the key is money. If it won't keep you fed or pay your rent, it's a hobby. A hobby could be the great passion of a person's life, the thing he or she lives to do, but it ain't a job.

That, as they say, is why they call jobs *work*.

But you're a writer, so you feel strongly about the nuances of words, and to you, "hobby" just doesn't cut it. "Hobby" implies "side gig," or "weekend fun." It does not imply sitting for hours at your computer, turning down invitations from friends, anxiously stringing together words on the page, and biting your nails while strangers read and judge your work.

Hey, there's that word *work* again.

Surely writing is work, if there ever was work. It's hard. It may be the only thing you want to do in life, but it's still really,

really hard. It requires discipline and study, and many failed attempts. You may labor at it on the side of your paid work, at night and on the weekends, but it is work. It feels like a job.

Sure, my devil's-advocate-on-my-shoulder, a mini-Mike, says, *but so can a hobby.*

Let me cite a relevant example in the form of a friend of ours, Phil. Phil and his wife Jo moved to New York from London a few years ago, because Jo is a cardiac surgeon and she got a big fellowship at a New York hospital. This required Phil to quit his job in London, and because of visa issues, he has not been able to secure a work permit in the States. As a result, he has had some time to pursue his hobbies—namely triathlons and photography. Because of these hobbies, not only is their apartment decorated with stunning, arty pictures he's taken, he looks ten years younger than his real age, and he's placing respectably in triathlons all over the world. He appears happy. His days are full.

And surely he had to study, apply amazing discipline, and endure many failed attempts in his quest for triathlon and arty photography success.

So: Hobby or job?

For some reason, I would agree with mini-Mike that Phil's "work" endeavors are hobbies. Why? For this critical reason: Phil doesn't aspire to get paid to do photography or triathlons. It would be nice, I'm sure, but that's not his goal.

For many, many writers—likely the kinds of writers who are reading this book—the goal is to make a living at writing.

Phil's photography and triathlons are "work," but they do not equate to a "job." He's just lucky enough to be able to fill his days with his hobbies.

So now we're getting somewhere. You can be doing work, and it can be difficult and tedious as well as rewarding and essential, but that doesn't make it a job.

Let's look at a more directly relevant example for a minute.

Julie Powell temped all day to pay her rent and buy groceries, but her hobby was cooking. For fun, she decided to cook her way through every single recipe in Julia Child's *Mastering the Art of French Cooking* in a single year and blog about her triumphs and failures. Her blog caught on like wildfire, got written up in *The New York Times*, and ultimately landed her a book contract and movie deal.

Okay: hobby or job?

It seems to me that the cooking and blogging were hobbies. Side gig. Weekend fun.

But having read her book, I know that the cooking and blogging were hard work. Some days she had to drag herself through the tasks. She got little sleep and schlepped all over the city to procure ingredients. *Work.*

But I'm a writer, so shouldn't I call it a job? I mean, she was writing, after all. And she did dream that her project would eventually become profitable, maybe even enough to allow her to quit temping.

I'm no hypocrite. Wasn't her blog a job?

Why am I so hesitant to call it that?

Probably because I am realizing as I write this that although it was work, it was not a job. I'm sure it *felt* like a job, just like my own writing sometimes feels like a thankless job.

But what I'm realizing is this: Until your writing pays you, it's work, not a job.

But mini-Mike and everyone else who tells you it's a hobby is also wrong.

Writing is NOT A HOBBY.

Writing is just too freaking hard to label it with a word that connotes relaxation and pleasure. It's *work*. It may not pay you—so you can agree that it's not a job, and let the other person feel like they're winning part of the argument—but for your own sense of self-worth, and for all the other writers out there toiling away on their novels in their spare time, be sure you call it work.

Postscript: I wrote the above for my book proposal, when I was still a bit clueless when it came to the idea of getting paid for your writing. After discussing this issue with other writer friends, I have discovered yet another wrinkle in this hobby/job/work conundrum. What if the writing pays you, but it doesn't pay *enough* to cover your rent or childcare, or anything else you need to function in order to finish the writing?

What if winning a triathlon involves a monetary prize?

Knotty problems, aren't they?

It seems to me that my original argument stands: If money is involved, it's a job, with all the stresses that come with a job—a boss/editor, deadlines, performance anxiety, and so on. It's just a poorly paid job that you need to supplement with other paid work. This is when you turn to the chapter on "getting a real job." I apologize in advance.

Sorry, BUT Yes, YOU DO HAVE TO "GET A REAL JOB"

$\mathcal{S}$ ince everyone is going to ask you what you're planning to do for money while you burn the midnight oil on your Great American Novel, you might as well devise an answer. And the truth is, you're going to *need* an answer, because that novel isn't going to pay your rent or feed you, certainly not while you're writing it on spec before sending it out to agents and editors, and probably not even after you get your (likely) slim advance, which pays you something like half a cent for every hour you slaved over it, and that's if you're lucky enough to get an advance at all.

But maybe you're not planning to be a novelist with a degree in English, like me. Maybe you love chemistry and poetry equally and plan to work in the former while dabbling in the latter. Maybe you want to be an engineer, or serve your country, or be a doctor without borders, but you think you might also want to write something, sometime—writing is in you, you feel it, but you haven't yet found your subject or genre.

Regardless of the kind of writer you might be or might become, the "real job" you get in the real world needs to be one that fosters your creative spirit and doesn't, as my professor put it, "kill your creative writing." This will mean different things for different writers.

For some writers, the surest way to inspiration will be to get a job that is not obviously writing oriented. Farmers, computer programmers, caterers, and police officers—to name just a few—might not appear to be on the fast track to publication, but every day they go to their jobs and gather details unique to their professions that would add a great deal of texture and authority to whatever kind of writing they eventually do. Michael Crichton's novels wouldn't be so thick with interesting scientific detail without his background in medicine. Arthur C. Clarke might not have written *2001: A Space Odyssey* had it not been for his time in the Royal Air Force and the British Interplanetary Society. For writers like these, the nonwriting career not only provides a stable income and professional security, it is the source of an amazing amount of usable material.

Some writers start in other professions that lead them to writing. This was the case for Jason Marshall, the husband of my longtime friend, writing buddy, and YARN cofounder Shannon. Jason has a Ph.D. from Cornell and, to quote his online bio, works as "a research scientist at the California Institute of Technology studying the infrared light emitted by starburst galaxies and quasars" (yeah, that was Greek to me, too). All that time spent with space and numbers turned out to be excellent preparation for his role as Math Dude at www.quickanddirtytips.com, where he offers a well-crafted podcast on how to "Make Math Easier," not to mention fun. He's also written a book as Math Dude.

Unlike me, who realized early that an all-consuming, full-time gig in academia would likely "kill my creative writing," writers like Marshall, Crichton, and many others fuel their writing with their full-time "real jobs." It's always seemed to me that these writers are lucky to have the salary and social standing that come with being able to say, "I am a doctor," or, "I am an astrophysicist," *and* to have the inspiration they receive daily on the job. They are writers who actually *wanted* to be something else, either in addition to being a writer, or before they ever dreamed they might be writers. But perhaps that's grass-is-greener envy talking. I also know that writing means just as much to those writers as it does to me, and to balance their "real jobs" with their writing, they surely have to give up much more in the way of spare time to get the writing done. Such is the case with my finance-guy friend with whom I've chatted about the sacrifices of the writing life.

It's also good for a writer to have wide-ranging interests so he can absorb all the information about those pursuits, digest them, and then use them in his writing. Some interests can lead to careers that work nicely with writing. For me, it's been crucial to carefully consider all of my interests and figure out how they relate to my writing. Of course, figuring that out has taken some trial and error. For instance, after college I did an internship in the curatorial department of the Guggenheim Museum because I was convinced that I would like to work in a museum or gallery, write for art magazines, *and* compose art-infused fiction; I thought these activities would produce the perfect synergy for me, creatively speaking. It took a summer of watching how the museum business works to show me that I probably didn't want to do that job after all. The art stayed in my fiction, but the rest went out the window as I tried other jobs and careers. It took me another four years to see that teaching worked quite nicely with my writing, and yet another eight to discover that editing also works well with my writing.

But for you, maybe baking scones for the café at Nordstrom and other eateries in your town, as a poet colleague of mine did, will lead to a scrumptious career writing cookbooks or gourmet mystery novels like those by Diane Mott Davidson or Nadia Gordon. It's impossible to tell where every job decision will take you. It's more important to remain flexible and open to the various possibilities life will throw in your path, since it's essential for a writer to absorb *life*, and work is very much a part of life. Without my experiences at the Guggenheim (and later as a nanny and a bookstore clerk, and later still as the manager of an olive oil store), my writing wouldn't be nearly as interesting—not because I ever wrote about characters in any of those precise settings, but because those jobs introduced me to people and places and events I wouldn't have otherwise known. In that way—and that way only I suspect—I guess I'm just like Michael Crichton.

When I first wrote this chapter, it contained a long list of the many different kinds of creativity and word-oriented professions a writer could embark upon that would pay the rent and potentially satisfy your itch for working with words so entirely that you wouldn't want to write your own novel or screenplay anymore. Then a wise reader of science fiction and historical fiction and nonfiction (hi, Mike!) pointed out that the young Isaac Asimovs and Stephen Jay Goulds reading this chapter would probably not see anything on that list for them, because most of the professions I discussed were for writer-readers who had majored in English, history, or a similarly "nonprofessional" subject. Since my guess is that a large number of this book's readers *will* be that kind of writer, I've moved all those professions to the "Appendix (Not the One You Had Out When You Were 10)." It's still important information, and you'll find at least a few suggestions for even the nonhumanities mind in there (like science writing: see the "Journalism" subheading). And since Isaac Asimov and Stephen Jay Gould were both professors themselves, writers of every stripe will be glad to know I've devoted a whole chapter to teaching as a profession—it's up next.

THOSE WHO CAN'T DO, *Teach*

It's amazing to me that this maxim persists, and is so often repeated either verbatim or by strong implication. "If you *can't* get published, maybe you can teach." Or, "Just because he doesn't have a book out doesn't mean he's not a great teacher." Or a collection of smug nods at dinner parties when you tell people you teach writing but have not yet published a novel.

Rest assured that anyone who thinks or says anything like this doesn't know what he's talking about. Let me give you a little ammunition to use against them in verbal battle, and also some information that I hope will be helpful as you make decisions about how to pursue your career as a writer.

For college teaching, the opposite of the above cliché is closer to the truth: *Those who have done, and done very well, teach.* This is true in almost every discipline. From my own experience in the field of writing, I can tell you that virtually no one these days can get a tenure-track college-level writing professorship without at least one published book on his résumé. If you have an MFA—or, even better, an MFA *and* a Ph.D. in English—and you don't yet have a published book or four, you might, as I did after grad school, be able to get a full-time renewable contract position teaching mostly freshman composition, but the competition for those positions is even stiffer now than it was for me almost a decade ago. My friends who teach and write in other humanities subjects, like art history (for which a Ph.D. is *de rigueur*), have had a similarly tough time in the twenty-first-century job market. Though they hadn't finished their first books by the time they landed their first assistant professorships, they *had* published or contributed to several journal articles. There seem to be a few more job openings for professorships in the sciences—for those who have an abiding love of biochemistry like Isaac Asimov, who taught at Boston University—plus the pay is better, but the best jobs are won by scholars with publication credits to their names.

The harsh realities of finding college-level teaching positions seem to be seeping into the public consciousness deeply enough that the "those who can't do, teach" allegation gets directed less at college professors than at the easier target: elementary and high school teachers. After all, you *can* get a job teaching K–12 without a published book or a stint at an internationally recognized lab; in fact, if you want to teach math or science, you're likely to have many job opportunities to teach high school and middle school right out of college. I've come to realize, though, that the "those who can't do" prejudice is part of an overarching respect problem for teachers. My mother was an elementary school principal, my great-aunt was a high school math teacher, my mother-in-law was a high school biology teacher, my dad taught business school classes, *and* I've been a college instructor myself, so I've been around a lot of teachers in my day. One of the classic laments of the teacher is how little people outside the profession think of what they do. Nonteachers cite long summer vacations and shorter working days as reasons why teachers are justly paid small salaries, or why teaching is supposedly a cushy job. Like they even know what they are talking about.

Okay, deep breath.

Despite all this social negativity, teaching—both college and K–12—is a wonderful profession for writers, and I feel so strongly about this that I've devoted a whole chapter to it. This is partly because I'm biased, and I'm happy to admit it. As a child of teachers, and having been one myself, I've been exposed to teaching's benefits more than I have for any other profession. But I also think teaching is an especially good career for a writer for many objective reasons.

For one thing, teaching *is* a profession. It's not just a job, like slinging coffee. It requires a higher degree: To teach most college subjects, you need a Ph.D.; for some subjects, like writing, you might only need a master's. To teach K–12, you need a master's in education in many states. In other states, you can get a special credential to start teaching with just your Bachelor of Arts, but if you want to advance in your career, you'll need a master's in a subject related to the one you teach (in those states, you don't have to get a master's in education—you could get an MFA to teach English).

As a profession, teaching offers plenty of room for growth within your classroom and beyond, and for yourself as a writer. Though you're likely to have a boss for most of your teaching career—unless you wind up as a principal or dean or superintendent—your classroom is very much your own. Even if you're teaching a set curriculum, as I have, you have lots of room (and necessity!) for improvisation and personalization. Your classroom, as many of my teacher friends have agreed, is your own little kingdom. And because it's a kingdom, it's not a desk—oh, you'll have a desk, but you'll rarely sit at it like you would in other professions. Teaching has a wonderful fluidity— walking around the classroom, going on field trips (if only to the library), clustering students into groups, and so on—that staves off a great deal of on-the-job boredom. Every day is different, not just because your lesson plans change, but because your students change and grow from month to month and year to year.

Whether you teach English, kindergarten, or trigonometry, you have the opportunity to immerse yourself daily in subjects that just might find their way into your writing (finger painting with five year olds just might inspire you to write a Caldecott winner!). If you teach writing, like I did, you'll teach what you do in your spare time: reading and writing. For many years, I found it phenomenally stimulating to teach my students what I knew about words. Being a teacher also made me more aware of my own reading and writing processes, and I found myself discovering and rediscovering techniques to share with my students. It was always rewarding to discover that some little trick that helped me could also help them. Plus, I also read about best practices of teaching writing, written by the pros in the field, from which I gleaned many helpful tips for my own writing. It was a virtuous circle that went round and round.

It's true, of course, that going round and round, even on one's favorite carnival ride, can get tiring, and it's certainly possible for academic writing to kill your creative writing. This possible conflict of interests is a judgment call only you can make about yourself and your work habits, but I would entreat you to give teaching a fair shot—if you're at all interested in it—before making your decision. I found that teaching the right subject actually increased my overall supply of creative juice. On a related note, as I mentioned in the last chapter, it's entirely possible that you'll find complete creative fulfillment as a teacher and won't need to write those poems, stories, or screenplays after all. There's only one way to find out!

Also keep in mind that teaching is one of the few professions in which you can take a leave of absence, often called a sabbatical, and return to the job without hurting your career. In fact, college professors are encouraged to take these breaks in order to work on their own scholarship so they can return to the classroom refreshed and renewed. In K–12 jobs, it's also possible to take periods off from teaching, as my mother did to raise two small children. After about ten years off, she returned to teaching when I was in fourth grade, and by the time I graduated college she was the principal of her own elementary school.

Like my mother, I've met some of my most like-minded, long-lasting friends through teaching. No one goes into this profession unless she believes strongly in education and the potential to change lives; teachers are thus optimistic, creative, and industrious in meeting their goals. Teachers tend to see and respect that the world is not black and white because we teach such a broad cross section of society.

Frequently, my colleagues were also aspiring writers, and I treasured the evenings we shared going out for dinner to talk about what it means to be a writer-teacher, to organize our schedules to accommodate both, and to fight the good fight. Because teaching *is* a good fight, maybe even *the* good fight. Whether a teacher is helping a fifth grader put a paragraph together or lecturing to college students about new strains of influenza, she is providing students with essential skills and knowledge and habits of mind that will make them better citizens.

And okay, yeah—even though this gets hurled at teachers as evidence that their profession is "easy" work—teaching does offer pretty decent hours. There is a very good reason why so many working mothers, even single working mothers, are teachers: the hours. If you're a mom, teaching K–12 puts you on the same academic year and same daily schedule as your kids. Everyone is in classrooms at the same time, and then when the kids are working on homework, the mom/teacher can be grading her papers.

The flaw in this thinking is that teaching as a profession requires many, many more work hours than what I just outlined. For one thing, grading and class prep always take longer than a kid's homework. I remember plenty of evenings and weekends during which my mother had to closet herself in her home office or go back to her classroom in order to get ready for the next day. K–12 teachers and college professors alike have to help with students' extracurricular activities, attend meetings and professional development seminars, and often attain higher degrees—*while* teaching full time—in order to move up the pay scale, and frankly, to avoid getting bored. This means *working* during those supposedly luxurious summer vacations. I don't know a single teacher who spent every summer just having fun.

Still, even with all that extra under-recognized work, teachers are more likely to have time left in a day, and year, for writing than those in professions with less flexible weekly hours that only allow the standard two-weeks-per-year American vacation. With careful scheduling, teaching can afford you time during the week and summer to do your writing, especially in the years before you procreate. It certainly did for me and many of my friends.

To be fair, the best, most flexible hours are offered to college instructors, not high school teachers. Let me just say it now: High school teachers are saints. I truly believe that facing five sets of thirty—or more!—students every single working day and instilling in them not just the lessons but a sense of maturity and self-esteem, is a calling. I have nothing but respect and admiration for high school teachers—that means you, Shannon Marshall (who, by the way, wrote a novel and much more while teaching high school English)—and I'm not sure I could ever do it myself.

College teaching was more my speed, because I only taught two or three days a week, though I should say that I was lucky enough to land a full-time gig right out of graduate school. Most recent grads with newly minted masters and Ph.D.s have to serve time as adjuncts. Adjuncts teach one or two classes at a university as part-time instructors, and the university doesn't have to pay all the benefits (health care, 401(k), and professional development) that they do for a full-time employee. To make ends meet, an adjunct usually has to teach a minimum of four classes at various institutions. This requires a decent amount of running around and prepping for different kinds of classes. On the other hand, it also means getting your foot in the door at a variety of colleges and universities, so that when a full-time opportunity to teach *does* come up, you have amassed the connections and goodwill that can really help you get the job. I know several people who have gone from adjunct to full time at colleges and universities.

Full-time positions like mine often require just as much teaching as adjuncts do, on paper at least. My contract was for four classes per semester, but I was quickly asked to take on other responsibilities, like writing a program handbook and later running the campus literary magazine, for which I was given "release time" from one of my classes. During most semesters, I taught three classes. It was still a lot, though, and it required an extraordinary amount of grading, which meant thinking about my students' writing more than my own. Plus, every semester I sat on or chaired at least two committees and attended many meetings and professional development seminars.

Even so, during my six years of full-time teaching, I managed to write two novels, several short stories, and a handful of essays, in addition to founding YARN. Not bad. It would have been very easy for me to allow my responsibilities on campus to balloon up to fill my entire schedule, but with my commitment to daily writing, which started way back in middle school, I was able to protect several mornings a week for my writing. And college teachers, unlike high school teachers, *do* get to use their quite long summer breaks for their scholarship; indeed, college professors are *expected* to write and publish in their fields.

The longer you're at a college, the more freedom your employers tend to give you. Though I was hired to teach exclusively freshman composition, I was eventually given opportunities to teach upper division creative writing workshops online and in classrooms. Remember what I said about teaching being a profession with opportunities for growth? Yeah. Pretty awesome. The same thing has happened with a close friend of mine who was hired as a full-time lecturer for composition but is now teaching fiction workshops as well.

Then there are the students. Let's not forget about them! You're probably a student right now. Picture your favorite teachers for a second. Are you smiling? I hope so. They smile when they think about you, too. And they really, really hope you send them an e-mail once in a while to update them on your adventures beyond their classrooms. Teaching you gave them extraordinary pleasure and was incredibly rewarding. Seeing you struggle, struggle, struggle, then *poof* get it. Or seeing you help your friends who were struggling, and thus help them teach the material. Or seeing you grow from an insecure freshman into an overconfident sophomore, and then into a mature senior. *You* are what motivates teachers to come back day after day, year after year.

Occasionally, your teachers might invite you to work with them, as I have with several former creative writing students who are now on the staff of YARN. That way, and in other ways, your teachers become colleagues and even friends. I recently reconnected with two of my former teachers, one from high school and one from college. They have known me as long as my closest friends, and though they are not the kinds of friends I'd go to a bar with, they are dear to my heart all the same. And I could tell they were happy to hear from me as well.

Teachers Without Classrooms

In addition to teaching in college or K–12, a whole world of teaching and education professions exists outside of the traditional classroom. These are also highly creative careers with room to work on your writing. For the sake of simplicity, I'll break them down into categories and talk about the kinds of jobs I know best.

Tutoring

You can do it through a service, like Kaplan, or at a writing center like the ones I describe in the "Appendix," or you can strike out on your own. Being an independent contractor will pay you a better hourly rate, but you'll probably have to pay for your own health benefits. As a private tutor for anything from the SAT to history papers, you can make up to $100 per hour or more, depending on the neighborhood you live in and the results you get. It takes time and a lot of afternoons posting your advertisement on neighborhood bulletin boards to build up a local clientele, but once your name is circulating among pleased parents, you could set up a very cushy gig for yourself. I tried this one summer and had four students and made good money. You can build your own schedule—conducive to the students' schedules, of course, which is easier in the summer when they aren't in school—and have as much free time as you want for your writing. However, you need to deliver results (higher scores, better grades) in order to build your business.

Private Advising

I have a friend who works privately with high school juniors and seniors on their college applications, helping them decide what schools to apply to, fill out their applications, and write their essays. Parents pay a lot of money for this kind of service, and you can make a lot. Plus, it sounds fun and comes with those precious flexible hours. If a job like this is appealing, you'll need some entry-level experience in your college's recruiting office, and maybe some tutoring experience as well.

Counseling and Advising in a School

So many kinds of counseling and advising services are currently offered by high schools and colleges, I can't possibly do them justice here. We're talking about everything from being the in-school therapist to the career counselor. In all of these jobs, you meet privately with students to coax them in the right direction, whether that's to take one more year of math in order to get into the right college, or to start looking for an internship. If you like one-on-one work with people and enjoy the feeling of helping others find and obtain what they want, this could be your line of work.

Specialists

Oh, how many specialists there are! Literacy specialists, special needs specialists, curriculum development specialists, art teachers, music teachers, and on and on. If you get your foot in the door of education or get the master's degree in education that so many states require to teach K–12, you just might find a specialty that suits you, and then you can flit from school to school teaching teachers and students what you know.

Administration

Administration can mean different things, but I'm going to use it here to mean the "boss" jobs in a school or college. These include deans, superintendents, principals, provosts, vice principals, and any other important-sounding person you've met in a school setting. These are not jobs you can generally get right out of graduate school, because institutions wisely hire people with a little field experience in the classroom to be in charge of those classrooms. But you can have your sights set on such a job quite early and work toward the job you want as you enjoy the kids for a few years. Administration jobs tend to come with more headaches than classroom teaching (being the boss always does), but if you think of yourself as a leader, it's something to consider. If you are very organized, like my mother was, the job doesn't even have to eat up all your time.

Other College Jobs

I have a friend who runs the study abroad office at the university where she also earned her Ph.D. In fact, she worked several jobs in the university at the same time that she was taking Ph.D. classes, then writing her dissertation, before finally inventing the position she now holds. She is accorded a great deal of respect in the institution and gets to hire her own staff. I have another friend whose husband is a musician who works in the fundraising office at a local university; it's decent money with excellent hours and benefits.

Colleges and universities have innumerable jobs like these, some of which you can actually start part time while you're still a college student. Have a look at the listings in the career office.

Teaching Abroad

Do you know anyone who's flown off to teach English in Vietnam for a few years? I do. They lived like kings on an amount of money that would have barely rented them a roach motel in the USA. If you like to travel and nothing is keeping you at home, you can find excellent opportunities to teach English (the language, not the literature) to aspirational kids and adults in countries all over the world, but in particular Southeast Asia and South America. You usually have to take a short course in how to teach English first, and then take a test. Once you do, you can get a job with part-time hours that pays you decent money (for that country) and affords you plenty of time to travel and do your creative work.

When I visited my good friend who was teaching in Saigon, I felt like she was living a life similar to the ex-pats of the 1920s in Paris: a cheap life with great food, plenty of beer, smart and interesting friends, and opportunities to work on her art and deeply experience a very exciting part of the world.

Some stay a year or two, some longer. If you want my two cents, this is a great job for a young person to gain some experience and time and have plenty of fun, but rare is the person who successfully expatriates permanently, managing to create a fully realized career and family life. Just read Hemingway or Fitzgerald. Another word of caution: While reading this chapter, my editor pointed out that sometimes teach-abroad opportunities are scams. It's wise to start somewhere a friend has gone before you, so you'll have someone to hook you into a legit teaching community, or be sure to do some research before you get on the plane! Your university's study abroad office would be a great place to start looking for information and alums who have gone this route in the past.

If you think you might like a life in education, I say go for it. There are so many avenues to explore, all of which will earn you friends, solid work experience, and time for your writing. Nothing to lose, everything to gain.

HATING YOUR
Best Friend

While I was waiting to hear back from the editors at Writer's Digest about their decision to publish this book, one of my closest writer friends landed a book deal for her first novel. Not just any deal—the kind of deal where five editors loved the book and fought over winning the privilege of publishing it.

Prior to the voicemail that delivered this news, I had been having a nice day. It was an unusually warm and sunny early spring afternoon, YARN had just received an exciting essay submission from a well-known writer, and I'd received a complimentary e-mail from an editor at a major YA publishing house about my editorial chutzpa. My daughter was happy, and I was bopping along to some classic *Glee* in my car on my way to do some grocery shopping.

Listening to her voicemail felt like falling off a cliff.

I was happy for her.

Really, I was.

I kept telling myself that.

Then I called my best friend from college and confessed otherwise.

"This sucks," I said.

"I know," she moaned in sympathy. Her own life had been pretty sucky lately, too, and she knew the essence and intensity of my pain.

There was little else to say.

I was much less happy for my good friend than I should have been. Had this happened a few years back, I would have experienced something that felt a lot like hate for her. I might even have said to myself, "I hate her." Fortunately, in that moment, at thirty-six years old, I did not hate her. Somewhere in my heart, I loved her. I loved how dedicated she'd been to that novel, which she started writing back when we were in grad school together. And I loved *her* and her steadfast friendship, ever since the day she'd traveled a long way to visit me when I was convalescing after getting my hips replaced (yes, I've had my hips replaced—long story for another time).

But it had taken me a lot of time and therapy to get to a place where I could tell the difference between the bad feelings I experienced that afternoon and the hate I would have mistaken it as years before. Oh, I'd been to Hateville. Several times, when, for instance:

- Two classmates in grad school placed first and second in *Zoetrope*'s annual big-deal short story contest.
- I discovered in grad school that several friends were receiving scholarship money from the department, funding that was directly proportional to how much the faculty liked their writing. I was getting $0 (like half my class, but still).
- Some of those same friends got personal introductions at cocktail and dinner parties—to which I was not invited—to those same faculty members' literary agents.
- Friends and classmates landed book deals for their novels and memoirs during and shortly after grad school with big-name publishing houses. Some of them have published several books by now, with sparkling, starred reviews from all the right places. In my lower moments, I have dwelt on the fact that many of those published writers are *younger* than I am, so they have a big freaking head start on their writing careers.

- A peer from the Community of Writers at Squaw Valley was featured on the front page of *The New York Times Book Review.*
- A classmate from grad school won a major award from an important institution of American letters.

Meanwhile, during the years when all those writer friends/acquaintances/classmates were enjoying the fruits of their labors, I was racking up rejections from literary journals, literary agents, and editors at publishing houses. The combination of their success and my failure was more than enough to make me hate them all.

And I hated them, I did. I was filled with hate. I hated the successful writers, and I *really* hated the unseen, unmet editors who couldn't see my talent.

Let me save you some expensive therapy and let you in on a secret: Anger and hate are actually cover emotions, masking a deeper and usually more painful emotion like fear or, in this case, envy.

One of my favorite essays, which I serendipitously read during my most toxic, hate-filled, and envious years, is the confessional, controversial "Envy," by Kathryn Chetkovich, about her unnamed writer boyfriend whose massive success made her miserable with envy (and when your boyfriend is Jonathan Franzen, as hers turned out to be, that level of envy is pretty understandable). This complex essay, about love and feminism and aging as well as envy, captured the essence of what I felt about friends who were finding success before I was, a kind of desperate longing that made me into an unhappy person I didn't want to be.

By the way, envy and jealousy are not the same thing, a distinction I learned from one of my creative writing students who chose the emotion "envy" out of a hat during a writing exercise. If you have a look on Dictionary.com, you'll find that *jealousy* is defined as "resentment against a rival, a person enjoying success or advantage." *Envy* is "a feeling of discontentment or covetousness with regard to another's advantages, success, possessions, etc." So jealousy is bad feelings toward the successful person, while envy is actually *the desire to possess* what someone else has. Whatever you think of religion, it seems worth noting that in Christianity, envy is one of the seven deadly sins, and in the larger Judeo-Christian tradition, covetousness is prohibited by the Tenth Commandment, so you can be sure that envy has been a primo source of misery since humans could see that the grass appeared greener in their neighbors' caves.

For a long time, I felt a deadly cocktail of jealousy *and* envy, and these feelings turned out to be much harder to deal with than the hate I initially thought I was feeling, because they were about *me*, not about all those people I purported to hate. *Oh my God,* I realized, *you mean there's something wrong with me, not them?*

But—and this is key—once I came to grips with the fact that my hate was really *envy* and therefore all about *me*, I could take the next logical step and realize that if it's about me, then I can control it.

More on that control soon.

First I need to talk about the ugly stepchild of envy: *schadenfreude.*

What a great word, right? Appropriately, I learned it in grad school, when I started avoiding the successful writers I "hated" and spending more time with my friends in Brooklyn who were getting Ph.D.s in art history instead.

Schadenfreude means taking pleasure in the misfortune of others.

So your friend just received a fiftieth rejection on her novel? True *schadenfreude* would mean being gleefully happy about her bad news, having a little celebration in your mind as you two-facedly pretend to be upset on her behalf. It's being truly happy that your friend has failed.

I never quite got to such a dark place, but I've slipped perilously close, and I bring it up so that you don't have to get there, either. All those times when I joined friends in bitching about the writing life and how freaking *hard* it is, and about how much we envied those writers who were no more talented than we were but more successful—all those times, I did take pleasure in the fact that I was in good company, which is a feeling *so close* to *schadenfreude* because it is pleasure in the company of others who are experiencing bad news similar to your own. But it's not quite *schadenfreude.* Call it extreme commiseration.

When things are going badly, of course it's easier to talk to a friend for whom things are also going badly than to talk to one for whom things are great. Commiseration feels good because it validates your own failure. If your friends are failing, your failure doesn't seem all that bad. You're still in league with your talented-but-not-yet-successful friends.

Comforting as all that commiseration feels, it will catch up to you because it is fueled by envy.

I woke up one morning a few years ago and didn't recognize myself. Growing up, I was the sort of person everyone used to describe as "sunny," always ready with a smile and an optimistic silver lining. But for months, I'd had a short fuse with everyone from my husband to my students. The only conversations that put me in an okay mood were commiserative. My thoughts constantly cycled back to my failures and my goals that increasingly felt like hollow pipe dreams for the future. My internal monologue was always negative, whether it was about me, my job, my writing, or anything else.

It had to stop.

So I went to therapy.

So cliché, I know.

But when you can't stand being inside your own head, something's got to give, and a well-employed cliché isn't going to hurt anybody.

One of the most important pieces of advice I got in therapy was a tip from cognitive behavioral therapy. My therapist called it "thought stopping." It worked like this: When I caught myself in a negative spiral of thought, I literally told myself to "stop," and then tried to do something specific to redirect my attention elsewhere. It's not unlike what I do with my toddler when she starts having a meltdown about the Elmo smoothie she can't have, and I divert her attention to the apple and Elmo stuffed animal she *can* have.

At the time I got this advice, I was starting to make YARN a reality, so my therapist suggested thinking about YARN, a project entirely under my control for which I could take tangible steps for tangible, pleasing results. She also recommended various other ways to get outside of my own head and pointed to studies that suggest that helping another person can actually shift the chemistry in your brain and make you happier. Maybe if I had volunteered at a soup kitchen or literacy center, my mood would have gone through the roof, but in the next few months I also got pregnant and had to plan an interstate move, so I only had time for small acts of kindness. I called a friend I knew was in need, helped a student I wasn't "required" to help, and other good deeds of that sort.

I also tried to notice the places where I was most prone to toxic thinking so that I could prevent the thinking from occurring in the first place. For me, the worst time of the day was my drive to and from work, close to an hour each way. Listening to music only conjured my publication dreams (getting The Call from my agent, quitting my day job, being on *Oprah*, and so on). Surprise, surprise! These little fantasy sessions just made me feel worse about the latest rejection in my inbox. Listening to the news made me feel generally depressed about the world. So I started listening to books on tape—and not just any books on tape. I listened to fast-paced mysteries and light, plot-driven novels that made me look forward to getting into the car so I could immerse myself in the activity that had gotten me into the book business to start with—*reading*. Not only was I behaving like a writer by reading in the car, I was effectively shutting out my toxic thought cycle and replacing it with fun stories. Win-win.

I'll be honest, though: All that practice thought stopping didn't stop me from falling off the cliff of toxic emotions that sunny spring afternoon when I listened to my friend's voicemail about her book deal. I'll admit I waded around in the envy for a while. As my other friend confirmed for me on the phone, it wasn't that I liked my writer friend less or didn't want her to be happy. It was just that I felt the intensity of my own bookless predicament a thousand times more. Plus, I'd lost one of my main partners in commiseration.

It helped me greatly to understand and embrace that difference, because even though it *hurt* to feel my booklessness, I knew I was in charge of getting over it. I'm not going to lie and say that I was able to wave my magic thought-stopping wand and make it all go away that day. There were plenty of good things for me to focus on that day, my adorable, happy toddler foremost among them. I couldn't focus on those things, though, and I found myself in a foul mood. For a while.

Since you're a shrewd reader, you've probably figured out that since I was waiting to hear back from editors about *this* book when I got the news about my friend, I got some good publication news of my own not too long after she got hers. While Writer's Digest's offer on this book definitely made me feel better about my writing life in general, you probably won't be surprised to hear that it wasn't a magic wand, either. After all, this book is not a novel—that hurdle is still in front of me. It *is* a strong positive sign, of course, just like getting into graduate school, or winning a scholarship to the Community of Writers at Squaw Valley, or founding YARN, or getting my first short story published. It's a sign that I am making progress on my writing journey. I am most certainly a tortoise, not a hare. Fortunately, tortoises live a long time.

The truth is that *writing* really helped heal that wound, and the others before it. By the time I got The Call from my agent about this book, I was no longer wallowing in my grief. I was focused on YARN and a brand-new novel to which I had committed with a pledge of devotion. *Writing* restored my sanity—writing, reading good writing, and editing exciting new writing.

I still need thought stopping for idle moments in my day when I am prone to envious thinking, but when I'm in front of the computer like I am now, filling the screen with the best of myself, I know that I am doing the right thing with my life. Other writers and their successes and failures fall away when I get immersed in my own writing, when I remember where I belong and why I love doing this. The mental equilibrium generated by my writing is the strongest fortification I have against the tyranny of envy. Writing reminds me that I write not just because I want to publish a book, but because it gives my life meaning.

So, too, does friendship, a fact I cannot overstate. My friend with the book deal dropped off the grid for a summer, so we haven't yet had a chance to speak at length about her exciting news. I find I cannot wait for her to return, though, so I can hear every detail and celebrate with her and look forward to our futures together.

After an inordinate amount of stressing, I finally sent this chapter to my friend, to see if she was comfortable with it. Luckily, she gave her seal of approval, and she also offered her own thoughts on the subject of envy. Not only do I think it's fitting to let her have the last word in this chapter, I think it would be useful for you all to know that she suffered on the road to publication, too. She knows all about envy, and she does a lovely job of summarizing this complicated state of being: "None of us are immune to it—it's a perfectly normal human emotion—and feeling it doesn't make you a bad person. Saying or doing something unkind is what you need to avoid! I dealt with jealous twinges by reminding myself that we all have our own paths as writers, and some people will get published before us, and others after. It's about doing the work we love, not about who gets what when. And you've really got to love writing, you've really got to be in this game because you *love* reading and writing. If not, don't do it; there are far, far easier ways of finding happiness and fulfillment."

HATING *Yourself*

The most poisonous side effect of the envy I described in the last chapter has been hating myself. This particular brand of hate usually visits me at night in the form of a maelstrom of negative thoughts that keeps me awake for many, many hours. Thoughts like: "I'm a bad writer," "I don't work hard enough," "I'm a bad friend for being so envious," and "People must think I'm so stupid for keeping at this thing that I clearly suck at." Beneath all that self-loathing are intense fears about my abilities as a writer and friend. If hating my friends is a cover for my deep, dark envy, then my self-hate is a mask for my most tender, personal insecurities.

Add to that insomnia and fear and envy a healthy dose of pointless hope—those daydreams about getting The Deal *next week* that keep not coming true—and I've felt like crawling into bed and never coming out.

It's probably time to admit that I have had two really excellent therapists in my adult life (all covered under health insurance, which is a reminder to make sure mental health is covered under whatever plan you pick). I mentioned one in the last chapter, and I had the other one when I was younger, not long after college. She used to tell me that it was sometimes productive to sit with my bad thoughts for a while, to feel them and the pain they inflicted, so that I would be prepared to move forward. This has proven to be good advice. I think there is some merit to pain: like "no pain, no gain." Just like at the gym, you have to actually *feel* the pain for it to affect you, for it to shape you in any way.

Why would you want pain to shape you, you smartly ask? It *hurts*. It can cause you to gain weight (too much junk food), or lose weight (nothing tastes good), and be generally Scrooge-like about everything and everyone.

For one thing, feeling your pain will give you a critical empathy you can pass along to your characters. I mean, do *you* want to read about a gorgeous person for whom everything has always gone according to plan? Me neither.

For another, feeling your pain will make you more resilient.

I know for sure that letting myself feel the pain that's resulted from the many disappointments chronicled in this book has made me a better and more resilient writer—a writer who isn't going to give up.

Resiliency doesn't get enough play in our culture. Overwhelmed as we are by a media machine that celebrates overnight success, reality shows starring people with zero talent or decorum, and sports heroes that peak at twenty-five or younger, it's hard to see the benefits of "slow and steady," let alone of weathering all the disappointments on the long road of the writing life.

Okay, I know that if someone had told me this when I was in high school, I probably wouldn't have listened. But I'm telling you now so that in a few years, in the likely event that you need a book to absorb your tears or withstand a few punches, you can open up this one.

Being a resilient writer means that you are able to change when you need to. My second therapist asked me, "You know how people say that the definition of insanity is doing the same thing over and over and expecting a different outcome?"

"Yes," I replied.

"Well," she went on, "that's not the actual definition of insanity, of course, but there is some truth to the idea."

We went on to discuss some changes I could make to my writing routine that would help me feel more in control of my destiny and less hateful of myself. Talking about it helped, and *making* the changes helped even more. At the time, those changes had to do with YARN and giving myself permission to take a break from novel writing to focus on the journal. Once I started plugging away at a literary endeavor that brought me some of the positive energy I so craved—even if it was in the form of compliments and collaboration on my editing rather than my writing—I found it much easier to sleep at night and turn off the spigot of painful thoughts.

You don't need a therapist to help you make changes like that, though. In fact, years before, my husband Mike helped me make what felt like a much more painful choice about my writing. I remember that we were at a diner having brunch one morning when, once again, I started complaining about my lack of success with publishing the short stories that comprised my MFA thesis.

"Maybe you're not writing the right kinds of stories," he said.

This simply did not compute. Like most writers, I wrote what my inner writer told me to write, what I was inspired to write. "What are you talking about?" I asked, irritated.

"Look at the writing you've had the most success with," he suggested. "What have you gotten published?"

"The Leonardo piece and the Vietnam piece," I replied, referring to the only historical fiction I'd ever written, and a short story set in Saigon.

"Right," he said. "Plus your essays, but I know you really want to write fiction. And aren't the rest of your stories about young women living in New York?"

I hated hearing that my writing boiled down to "women in the city." Yuck. "They're about more than that," I chafed. After all, one of those so-called "women in the city" stories had gotten me a scholarship to the Community of Writers at Squaw Valley!

"I'm not saying those are bad stories, or that they aren't as well written," he said. "I'm just trying to say that there are a lot of them out there, and so it's harder to get them published."

"Oh," I said, backing off, because I could kind of see his point. This was the heyday of chick lit and *Sex and the City*, after all, and even though my stories had a distinctive art and art-historical quality to them, they could definitely be categorized as "women in the city" stories, especially to an editor who was pressed for time and would only read a few lines before deciding if she was going to read more. Maybe I needed to make a few changes based on this reality.

"If I were you," he said, "I would focus more on the stories that set you apart."

"Those are hard to get published, too," I said, not one to back down easily.

"Nothing is easy to get published," he agreed. "But I just think you should focus on what's brought you the most success already. You obviously do that well."

I did not go on to write a novel of historical fiction, or one set in a foreign land, but I did take his point, and I found other ways to implement his advice, like writing the mystery novel that got me my agent, and eventually focusing on the essay writing he mentioned—which, I have to admit, did get me my first book deal.

A willingness to listen to smart advice and a willingness to make changes in my writing have been the only ways to help me move beyond the crippling effects of hating myself. Though others have helped me see the kinds of changes I need to make, it's usually me that comes up with the precise changes, a process that is very empowering. When I am designing solutions to my problems, I feel my pain less and less and begin instead to feel stronger, more capable, and in charge of my fate.

WRITING FOR *Pleasure*

*I*n virtually every FAQ page or interview I've read about a published writer, I've seen the same thing: "If you're writing just to get published, you won't be writing for very long, and you almost certainly won't get published. You have to write for pleasure."

Yeah, right. Easy for them to say—they've gotten their novels published!

Unfortunately, like all that depressing advice I mentioned in the introduction, this little gem is true as well. One of the hardest and most essential lessons a writer can learn is to write in the full knowledge that It—the book deal, the big-budget movie, the collection of poems—may never happen. There is no point in pretending that It *will* happen, that It might even happen tomorrow; I've done that, and it only makes the stark reality all the worse. I have a friend who basically told herself that It wasn't going to happen. Ever. But she worked on her novel anyway. For years. She sent it to agents, though she told herself It wasn't going to happen. When she finally got an agent, who sent it to editors, she braced herself for disappointment. She wasn't disappointed (yes, I'm being ironic). She had to go back and work on the novel some more. Then her agent sent the book out again, and *bam! It* happened.

While I have my superstitious moments, I certainly don't believe that my friend's It's-not-going-to-happen attitude actually made It happen. What I did notice, however, is that she was a little calmer about the whole process than I was. A little less up and down. For a long time, she felt like publication was so far in her future that she wasn't thinking about it at all while she wrote her novel. She wrote her novel because the story was inside of her, begging to come out. She wrote and rewrote to teach herself how to write a novel.

She wrote, if not for pleasure exactly, then for herself.

On some level, we are all writing for ourselves. Since first novels, stories, and poems are almost always written on spec, without any promise of publication, when we write them, we are writing a story that lives only in us. Until we show it to people, it exists only in our heads and our computers. The act of writing it might feel like scratching an itch, or screaming out loud, or pulling out a tapeworm, but when we write, read, and rewrite it, we're doing it for ourselves. Nobody is making us do it. We are our own first audience, and we need to be happy with our work before anyone else is.

When I'm in the act of writing, I really do write for myself, and little interferes with that. My doubts only surface when I am away from my writing, and I find myself dwelling not on the writing itself but what will come of the writing and what will happen to me if It never happens. And then, as I've discussed elsewhere in this book, all that stuff will sometimes keep me from sitting down to write at all.

Other writers worry about publication, their audience, the anxiety of influence, and a thousand other things *while* they are writing. They have the phenomenally difficult task of learning to shut off those obnoxious voices while they listen to the story inside them that needs to be told.

Paradoxically, I find it comforting to know that even published writers face these same problems. Even if you already have one, two, or even four or five published books, there is no guarantee that your next one is going to find its way to the bookstore shelves. Writers lucky enough to be under contract for multiple books also have to accept clauses that allow publishers to back out of the next book if they feel that the author has not delivered what he'd promised. Most writers don't have multibook deals; instead they must give their publishers a right of first refusal, which means that the publisher who published your most recent book gets to read the new one first and decide if they are going to make an offer before your agent can send it elsewhere. Some writers of published novels don't even have that; it's on-spec writing, book after book.

I have a friend who published two excellent novels that did quite well, but her third novel never sold. She's working on a fourth. One of my early mentors, who published many books in her esteemed career, was never able to sell one of her most beloved novels, a book she worked on for years and years. Because it was such a departure from her other work, her own editor and others didn't quite know what to do with it.

Which means that all of us—even the published novelists—are on tenterhooks, waiting and longing and wondering what will happen next.

For me, the only antidote to all this angst has been to focus on *writing*, which is what I think all those published writers are really trying to tell us in those FAQ pages and interviews. Since they *are* published, they know better than we do that even publication doesn't come with any promises. Publication will not, as Anne Lamott says in *Bird by Bird*, "change your life or solve your problems," nor will it "make you more confident or more beautiful, and it will probably not make you any richer."

The $64,000 question, then, is how do you do it? How do you learn to write just for the sake of writing? Maybe even—dare I say it—for *pleasure*?

This book is full of potential answers, littered throughout the other chapters: Come at it from the side, leave your ego at the door, buy a planner, play with your words, be willing to change, learn to thought stop and divert your attention to something you can control.

But before you can do any of those things, I think you need to ask yourself why you want to write in the first place.

Did you just ask yourself?

(I'm waiting.)

Okay.

If your answer was something like, "Because I can't imagine *not* doing it," then you're on to something. You know on some level that writing is just *in* you, like your intestines or your skeleton, and you wouldn't be you without it.

The rest is discipline. Put one word in front of the other, and try to forget about the rest of it. This is one-day-at-a-time, one-word-at-a-time, one-sentence/paragraph/story-at-a-time work. *Work.* It may not be your job, but it sure as heck is work. It's the work *worth doing.*

I'm still figuring out how to do the work and keep the demons at bay, and I suspect that I will be forever, no matter how many books I publish. I'm also trying to keep in mind that the writing life isn't just about getting published. It's about living my life with a constant and deep love and respect for written words—reading them, discussing them, and sharing them with friends. I realize that *sharing* has been a recurring theme of this book. It cropped up while I was writing about soap operas, and SARK, and the team effort of published writing, and you'll see it again in the last chapter. Really, it's been an underlying theme in everything I've had to say about writing. Sharing. It's such an intimate form of communication—it's reaching out and offering a part of yourself; it's asking to be heard, to be seen.

Sometimes it's enough for me to be heard by myself. I use writing as a form of thinking on the page. In a day that is full of the noise of family and friends, work, and everything else, it is such a joy to be able to sit down *with myself* and be heard *by* myself. Sometimes I crave more, and so I ask a writing buddy to read what I've written, and then that often grows into a desire to share what I've written with a wider audience. But the *pleasure*—and it's the deepest, most real pleasure I have known in writing—is first and foremost the quiet and satisfying communication with myself. It's been enough to sustain me for many years, and I'm going to try and remember it in the years to come.

GETTING PUBLISHED,
Big Time AND
Small Time

I remember when my first story was accepted at a journal. It was on a sticky afternoon late in the summer I turned thirty, a birthday that had surprised me with the tidal wave of anger and angst it brought along with it. For weeks, I'd felt irritable and mopey, and as my birthday approached, I started to realize exactly why: I was going to turn the big three-oh without a single publication credit to my name.

That had not been part of the plan.

I had planned to be on *Oprah* by the time I was twenty-five.

So the birthday came and went, and once it was behind me, I tried to forget about what was increasingly starting to feel like the failure of my writing career.

A month later, I opened my laptop on a hot August afternoon to prep for the classes I'd be teaching in a few weeks, and I saw the e-mail in my inbox. In the Subject line was the title of a short story I'd sent to the journal, and in the From line was a man's name I didn't recognize, but it wasn't the usually fateful "editors@journalabouttorejectyou.com." My hand shaking with excitement, I clicked on the message. It was from a new editor at the journal telling me how much he liked my story and asking if I'd be willing to do some edits for him?

Of course! Yippee!

Talk about an excellent belated birthday present.

That same summer I also had a short essay accepted at an academic journal.

And you know what? I can't remember which came first—the story or the essay. Strange, isn't it, how the mind plays tricks with memories. Sometimes this is a defense mechanism to protect us from things too painful to dwell upon. Sometimes, though, the details of how we finally came to attain a much-longed-for goal cease to be important. Given how dearly I've held fiction for so long, you'd think the details of which success came first would be firmly implanted in my brain. But they're not. Along those same lines, it's amazing to me that I very rarely replay in my mind The Call from my agent telling me a book of mine had sold, whereas before I got The Call, I spent years imagining it in minute detail—where I'd be, who I'd tell (after, of course, the hysterical calls to my husband and parents), the door I'd fling open to "sound my barbaric yawp" (thanks, Walt Whitman), and the champagne I'd drink that night.

Speaking of publication realities being less important than you would have predicted, did you notice when you read the table of contents that this chapter and the next one are the only two in this book that are all about publication?

Surprised me, too. I would have thought that in a writer's life, publication was supposed to be the biggest, most important thing. I would have thought more words would be dedicated to it in a book of this kind.

Until I actually started writing the book.

But. This *is* a book about writing and being a writer, so I would be remiss if I didn't tell you a little something about how the whole publication thing works. So this chapter will focus on how to put your best foot forward to editors and agents and publishers, and the next will focus on what happens once something gets accepted. I'll be writing that one *as I learn* about book publishing, as this very book moves through the process at Writer's Digest Books.

I'm going to start with how to get a short piece of writing—a few poems, say, or an essay, or a short story—published in a literary journal; *however, if you're writing a novel and are interested in querying agents, you should still read this section* because so much of this process will also apply to finding an agent, and I'm going to refer back to this first part in the section about novels. Also, it doesn't hurt to rack up a few publication credits for short pieces in magazines and journals before you try to launch your career as a novelist. It will show that you're serious about writing and will also contribute to the herd mentality described later in this chapter.

The first and most important thing is to have a polished, fully revised, and proofread piece of writing of which you are very proud. You've worked hard on it, you think it's unique, and it's ready to go. The next thing is to figure out where to send it. If you're writing in a genre, your job is much easier—only a handful of journals specialize in mysteries, for instance, and a few handfuls focus on fantasy and science fiction, and half a handful concentrate on YA (be sure to check out YARN!). If you're writing adult literary fiction, your options are many and varied.

Finding the Right Journals

Almost all literary journals have online presences now, and I wish they'd had them when I was starting out! If I were compiling my list of journals today, I would start with the Council of Literary Magazines and Presses (CLMP.org), which provides a long list of journals that are members of the council with links to all their websites. Tried-and-true books like the annual Writer's Market series, some of which also offer online subscriptions, will provide a brief summary of thousands of journals and what they are looking for, because believe it or not, not all literary journals are created equal. At some big-name journals, like *Granta* and *The Paris Review*, a young unknown writer doesn't really stand a chance of getting a story published when they are competing with the likes of Joyce Carol Oates and Russell Banks. I still occasionally submit to these journals, because what the heck, right? One of them, *Zoetrope*, has even written me some very encouraging rejections, with specific comments on the story and handwritten notes asking me to send more. Oh, those handwritten notes—nothing is more heartening to a writer! And believe me, now that I'm an editor who is inundated with submissions, I know an editor would *never* encourage someone she didn't feel strongly about. So take those compliments where you find them.

If you're like me, though, these websites and books can feel more than a little overwhelming—so many options! If you prefer a more curated selection, have a look at your very own bookshelf. One of the best publication tips I ever received was to pluck books off my own shelves and look to see where the stories were originally published. (This technique also works for finding an agent, but more on that later.) I tried this with a few books that contained stories I thought were a little like mine. From there, I vectored out, clicking on other journals where writers I liked had published, or on the websites of writer friends of writers I liked. I started to see relationships between certain writers and journals in bibliographies and FAQ and links pages online, and with a few afternoon click-fests, I was able to compile a solid list of places to send my work. I also went to my university and local public libraries to flip through as many of the journals as possible, just to verify that, yes, they do publish work like mine.

I'm not going to lie, though—it helps to have a connection. My first published short story was edited by people connected to the Columbia MFA program I attended.

Which Brings Me to the Cover Letter

If you have a connection to the editors or anything else about the journal, say so in the cover letter—if you went to the same summer camp, if you saw a panel where one of the editors spoke, if your English teacher knows one of the editors, whatever. It doesn't matter what the connection is. Mention it. It won't guarantee your publication, but it might get you into a different pile of slush from the rest— the "read more carefully" pile.

A well-tailored compliment also helps, especially if you do not have a connection. These journals want to know that you've actually picked up and read some of their stuff. So tell them how much you liked Kerri Majors's essay in last winter's issue. They will take you more seriously.

For journals, short and sweet does the trick for cover letters: a few sentences to two paragraphs at most! In the first paragraph, introduce yourself and attempt to make as personal a connection as possible between you and the journal (the compliment, or the I-met-your-poetry-editor comment). In the second paragraph, include a brief bio with the best of your credentials—editor of your high school paper, founder of a literary society in your dorm, voted most likely to wear black and drink espresso. Keep in mind that no one is going to hold it against you if you've never been published before. Your work is still going to be read. At YARN, everyone is read by a minimum of two readers, and we're pretty typical. A list of credentials will mainly make the readers pause and think, "Oh, other people think this writer is cool," which tends to put them in a friendly frame of mind.

And as one writing teacher at Columbia once said to my class, "Editors are like sheep. Followers."

While the editor in me smarts at this remark, I have to admit there is some truth to it. For me, though, it's not so much that I am likely to accept a piece if the writer has been published in other impressive journals; it's more that if I am on the fence about publishing a piece, I might look back at the writer's list of credentials and think, "Hmm, well, if she was published for three years in her school's art zine, maybe I should give this the benefit of the doubt." *Baa*.

The Most Important Step: Read the Submission Guidelines

Make sure you follow them to the letter. Nothing irks us anal-retentive literature types more than misfollowed directions. If the journal tells you to paste the story into the body of your e-mail, don't send an attachment! If they prefer snail mail, suck it up, purchase the postage, and remember that in the dark ages fifteen years ago, all writers had to submit almost everything by snail mail, and it wasn't cheap. Paper is expensive, *and* you had to include a self-addressed, stamped envelope (SASE) for the inevitable rejection, which always made the whole process feel like a depressing forgone conclusion. I find e-mail and submission managers to be much more optimistic.

So do what the journal asks, prep your work accordingly, and send.

Then Forget About It (The Hardest Part)

You spend all this time with your story or poem or essay, getting it ready like it's going to summer camp, then you send it out into the world. Yikes. Feeling a little sympathy for your parents?

The only way I have been able to truly get my mind off the submitted story is to work on the next story, novel, or whatever I'm writing. That way, when I sit down at my desk for my scheduled writing time, I won't be as tempted to revisit the websites of the journals to which I've sent pieces, trying to telepathically communicate that they should publish my story.

Simultaneous Submissions

In case you're not sure what "simultaneous submissions" means, it's submitting your story simultaneously to multiple journals at the same time. Some journals will say, "No simultaneous submissions" in their guidelines. As another of my former writing teachers at Columbia said, "They have a hell of a lot of nerve requesting no simultaneous submissions. If you really only sent one story out to one journal at a time, you'd never get published before you die." Truer words were never spoken.

Most writers I know just ignore prohibitions of "no simultaneous submissions." The overwhelming likelihood is that you're going to get rejected anyway. In the unlikely event that you get accepted somewhere else before the no-simultaneous place, just write a quick note to the stricter journal saying with profuse apologies, "I didn't realize that the other journal was still considering my work. Please withdraw my story from your queue." Trust me, unless you are J.K. Rowling, they won't care. And anyway, the vast majority of journals accept and even encourage simultaneous submissions because the editors are writers, too, and they understand the quandary we are all in together.

Another word about multiple submissions: Since you absolutely *should* send out each story/poem/essay to more than one journal at a time, come up with a way to track your acceptances and rejections. I use an old-fashioned table in a Word document that's gotten completely out of hand with journals in the far left column and the titles of my stories across the top horizontal row. Where the story meets the journal in the grid, I write down when I sent the story, when I heard back from them, and what they said. Now that I know how to use Excel I'll probably have to redesign this table using an Excel spreadsheet, but instead I might look into a software program with searchable contacts and data fields designed for writers to keep track of journals and stories.

Be Mechanical About All of This

Make like a tin man with no heart: When your rejection letters arrive, file them away in a folder you don't have to look at unless you need to open it, then just send the story out to the next journal on your list. I generally send each story out to ten journals at a time. This process works on two levels: 1) implementing a dispassionate, pragmatic assembly line process makes it less likely you're going to get personally invested in every single rejection letter, and 2) it helps you do the ultimately very boring and, yes, mechanical work of sending out your writing.

Be Open to Revisions

I'm going to give it to you straight as the editor of YARN: Be open to making changes to your work if the editor asks for it, even if he hasn't yet promised to publish you. I can't tell you how off-putting it is to read a piece I think has potential, then go to the trouble of e-mailing comments to a writer, only to have her either ignore my e-mail or refuse to even try. I mean, didn't she want to get published? More importantly, didn't she want to improve her writing?

To be fair, the majority of writers from whom I've asked for revisions, teen writers and established writers alike, have cheerfully agreed to give it a go. It can be a fun process, in fact, in which the writer gets to work on her craft and receive snaps from an editor for doing so. I love working with writers on their stories. It's truly a joy to see a good story become great, and I love to tell writers what they are doing well, and to use those strengths to help them improve what needs improving—and then to be pleasantly surprised at the ways in which they implement my advice.

Of course, this revision process doesn't always have a happy publication ending. Several times, I've asked writers to revise—sometimes more than once—and the story still doesn't quite work well enough for YARN. I'm always so impressed when those writers thank me anyway, telling me how much they learned about writing from our exchanges.

I've been that writer, too. I've been asked to revise my work five times without the promise of acceptance. Two of those five times, for a story and an essay, I was indeed accepted at the end of the revision process. One time, my essay was still rejected.

One time was for a novel, and I was asked for revisions by an agent whose associate later became my agent (not bad—more on that in a bit).

The most heartbreaking time, I was asked for revisions by an editor at a major publishing house who liked a draft of my YA novel. From her first conversation with my agent, it looked like she was going to buy my book. Then she invited me to her office—*Her office! What a thrill!*—and told me all the things she thought I might want to change about the book "noncontractually."

My heart sank, literally. I had to pick it up off the floor from the bloody puddle it had created between my boots. I had heard stories like this one. In fact, before meeting with this editor, I'd had lunch with a good friend and we had actually discussed a mutual friend who had been asked once for a noncontractual revision. He'd toiled and toiled on his manuscript, only to have it rejected.

I was full of a sense of foreboding, but also of hope, as I undertook my own revision. I would not have done it at all had the editor's comments not resonated with me, but they had—I thought they were smart and very doable. For the next two months, all I did was work to produce a revised novel that I was happy with, and that my agent called "much richer."

The editor didn't agree.

Yes, indeed, sometimes this whole writing thing downright sucks.

On the upside, though, I had a much improved novel on my hands. The editor's comments had also crystallized a writing weakness that I realized I'd been hearing in one form or another for several years, especially on my novels: My protagonists needed to be more person-ally invested in the plot; they were too often observers, not drivers, of action. Because of her comments, I know to be on the lookout for this issue in everything I write, so I can head it off at the pass.

Trust me, it took a long time to be able to see those silver threads lining the big dark cloud that hung over my head and soaked me to the bone every day for months and months.

I wouldn't go back and do it differently, though. Truly, what choice did I have? An editor at a major house liked my book! Did I want to get published or not?

I think by now you know the answer to that question.

What If You're Looking for an Agent?

Now that I've already skipped ahead and shared that memory of my brush with a big trade publisher, now is a good time to start talking about getting a book published. The big time.

I did a quickie rendition of how I found my agent earlier in "Eaves-dropping," but since I know that this is the kind of story writers *thrive on* (me too!), I'll give you my full-blown story here, because I think it summarizes and animates much of the advice I've given above and applies it to the find-an-agent process.

Once I finished the third draft of my mystery novel, I knew I was ready to start looking for an agent. The manuscript was in good shape; I'd followed all my own advice from the first part of this book. To find an agent, I did several things.

I opened a file I'd been keeping on my computer of agents I'd heard about, either through friends, panels I'd attended at Colum-bia, or articles I'd read online. Since virtually every literary agency has a website, it was very easy to locate detailed information about the agents in my file. Some got put on the "Send To" list, and others

I tossed out, because it turned out they were looking for cookbooks or erotica, which was not what I had written.

I had also been keeping a running list of agents who were thanked on the Acknowledgments page of all the mysteries I'd read that were a little like mine, as well as some of the literary fiction I admired. Then I did the same online research on those agents, adding some to the "Send To" list and discarding others.

I also networked by going to the New England Crime Bake, the official conference of the New England chapter of the Mystery Writers of America, which also served as an excellent resource for finding agents at locally offered panels, readings, and discussions. At the Crime Bake, not only did I get myself on the list for the official "Agent Pitch" opportunity, but for three days, I was in a room full of famous mystery writers and their editors and agents. There was plenty of time for schmoozing! I just had to perfect my "elevator speech"—you know, the two-minute spiel about my book designed to get an agent to say, "Wow, I've got to read this"—and then get up the courage to present it.

I had some good luck at the Crime Bake. The agent to whom I officially pitched my novel said I should "send it right away," leaving me fairly breathless with his enthusiasm. At coffee breaks and lunches designed for mingling, I informally pitched to a few other agents whose professional biographies suggested they might be good matches for my novel, and in all, I came away with at least five agents who said they would be happy to read my book.

When I got home, I checked the agency submission guidelines and prepped my materials accordingly. I carefully composed cover letters to the agents, each of which were a bit more detailed than the letters I sent to literary journals. So much more was at stake here than the fate of one story. An agent was a person who would hopefully represent me for my entire career! In the first paragraph, I was as detailed and personal as possible, explaining how I knew the agent and also discussing one or two authors they represented and why I admired them. In the next paragraph, I offered a slightly longer biography with my credentials, including all the publications that had already published my short works, and thanked them for their time before signing my name.

But I was really holding out hope for one agent in particular: Ann Rittenberg.

When I was fresh out of college and living in Brooklyn while writing my first novel, I interned for Ann at her home office, mainly reading the slush and sending rejections. In the process, I saw that I was not cut out to become an agent myself, but more importantly, Ann became a mentor to me. She doled out no-nonsense advice about publishing (and dating and having children), and she left the door wide open for me to submit my own work to her when I was ready.

Some months after I finished my internship and she moved her office to Manhattan, I was ready to show her my first novel. I was disappointed by her reaction, which boiled down to: "You have potential, but you still need to work on your craft." She was right, though.

Years later, I sent her my romance novel. She agreed to read the first part of that book, too, and in retrospect, I realize what a big show of faith that really was. She's an incredibly busy woman. When I asked her to read it, I acknowledged that she didn't usually represent romance, and I was open to suggestions she might have for other agents to try. She read my pages and politely agreed that it wasn't her cup of tea, but suggested I try three colleagues of hers. It still didn't work out, but the experience kept me in touch with Ann and kept me agile in the whole publication game.

After all that history, when it came to the mystery novel, I figured This Was It. Ann represented many mystery writers, including some highly acclaimed and best-selling authors, and I wanted to be on her list. My e-mail to her asked after her three daughters and relayed my excitement about the latest successes of her biggest authors.

She actually *called* me on the phone when she got my query letter to tell me how excited she was to read the book and how my plot and character synopsis really "spoke to" her. I danced a jig in my office after that phone call.

A little while after I sent her the manuscript, I saw a big, fat, book-sized package in my mailbox with Ann's agency mailing label on it.

This was not good.

Unable to wait until I got into the house to read the bad news, I tore open the white mailer and read the letter that covered the rubber-banded pages of my novel. She was still enthused about the book and gave me a few ego-boosting compliments on the main character, the prose, and the story. Then she gave me some concise and wise suggestions with an invitation to call her if I wanted to discuss it in more detail.

Whew.

That wasn't nearly as horrible as the package in my mailbox had implied. There was still hope.

I called her the next day and took notes as she spoke. Everything she said made perfect sense to me, and I could tell she wanted to read it again once I'd revised it.

Sure, I was disappointed that she didn't offer to represent me before I did the revisions. But still, this was a much more solid lead than any I'd gotten so far. As the months had gone by, I'd collected quite a nice stack of rejection letters from other agents, including the one who seemed so excited at the Crime Bake. Some of the letters were very apologetic and personal, and others were to-be-expected form letters. But I tried to be as mechanical about the process as possible, filing away each rejection and sending the book out to the next agent on my list. After an initial batch of ten, I generally tried to send the book out to five agents at a time.

I revised the book with Ann's comments in mind. It took a few months, since her suggestions affected the entire manuscript, but I was excited by them. With every change, I sensed the novel getting stronger, and I sent it back to her full of hope and, I admit, tentative confidence.

Then a month ticked by.

And another.

And then another four.

Meanwhile I wrote a whole other book, a YA paranormal, partly because this new story was burning a hole in my brain and partly because it was the best possible distraction from my disappointment about all the rejections of the mystery.

I had almost given up on the mystery when I got a call one August morning from Ann.

You can imagine what my heart did in my chest. She wouldn't be calling if it wasn't good news!

Right?

I listened as she apologized for how long it had taken her to get back to me, though she had excellent reasons, the most germane being that *everyone in her office had read and loved my book*, including their summer intern and her associate, Penn Whaling, who had *really* loved the book and *really* wanted to represent it.

!!!!

Would I be interested in Penn representing me? Ann oozed praise about Penn, saying she was a very smart young woman and the best reader she knew. She said Penn knew the kinds of editors who would be most interested in my novel, and she thought Penn would be the best fit for me.

Was I interested?

"That sounds great, Ann! Definitely tell Penn to call me." I think I just barely kept the tears of joy and relief out of my voice.

I had just enough time to run screaming to my husband with the good news, and for us to do a little happy dance together in the hall, before Penn called me to tell me how excited she was to get down to business.

She just had a few suggestions for the book before she showed it to editors.

Of course.

But this time, a contract was also coming in the mail.

It's been a long road for me and Penn to a book contract for this very book. The economic meltdown of 2008 didn't help sell the mystery, which was about a Gatsby-esque tycoon. But let me just tell you how grateful I am that she has been so loyal and so prepared for all the twists and turns I've thrown at her over the years. She initially signed on for a mystery, but she gamely read and got excited about that YA paranormal, as well as this book about writing. I feel lucky to have an agent who looks at the total package of me as a writer and an editor of YARN, and wants to support that career.

Those are things to consider as you look at agents. Do they have long-standing relationships with their writers? Do they seem to understand you and your writing? Do they regard publishing with the serene, tortoise-not-hare attitude that will be necessary to help calm you down as you're climbing the walls waiting for answers from editors?

Hitting the Jackpot

As you've no doubt gathered from the adventures I've relayed above, getting from your research on agents to an actual book deal can take a long time. The book business is full of stories of writers who were rewarded for their waiting, like Meg Cabot, who will tell you on her website that she waited three years before finding an agent, and another year before her agent sold her first book. A friend of mine waited eighteen months before her agent sent her novel out to a second wave of editors. After the first round said no, she revised the book a bit, waited, and *boom!* A sale.

Once you find your agent, she has to go through almost exactly the same process to find the right editor. Of course, your agent will have a handful of first-choice editors already in mind when she agrees to represent your book. If my experience and those of my close writer-friends are any indication, your agent will be sending your book to ten or even twenty editors on a first round, so she'll probably have to do a bit of research of her own, in her rolodex and databases, looking for just the right editors for your book, while you toil away on those final edits to the manuscript that she suggested.

Then, just like you, she'll send out a wave of pitch letters to the editors. Unlike you, though, she is a member of the publishing club, so she'll have a much faster response rate and much higher rate of "Yes, please send me that intriguing manuscript to read" responses than you did when you were looking for agents.

And then, as you and your agent wait and try your best not to think about what's happening, your book is moving through the acquisition process at a dozen or so publishing houses.

At some houses, your book won't get far, and you'll get a rejection from the editor to whom your agent sent the book. My agent forwarded me all those e-mails, and we had a good laugh about some of them: One of the editors for this book called it *This Is Not a Writing Manuel*, which prompted witty Penn to say it made her "picture *un hombre en un sombrero con una pluma.*" Another addressed her as "Agent Whaling," which she said made her feel like she was in the FBI. See what I mean about picking the right agent?

But if the editor is intrigued by your project, your book will go deeper into the publishing machine.

I've learned recently that every publishing house moves differently in their acquisition process. Some houses have an acquisitions editor whose sole job is to vet new projects and pitch them to an editorial board that includes other editors as well as sales and marketing people who provide input about the salability of your book. If your book is approved, the acquisitions editor will contact your agent with an offer. Then you'll never hear from that editor again; you and your book will be handed over to the contracts manager who fashions your contract and handles any negotiation on that document, and you'll be assigned a content editor who will work with you on shaping your book for publication. At other houses, the editor to whom your agent sent your book will be the all-purpose editor of your book—it's that editor who will pitch your book to the in-house review board (again including sales and marketing people), edit the content of your book, and stay with you until your book hits the shelves. More on all that in the next chapter.

No matter which kind of editor acquires and edits your book, The Offer starts with The Call from your agent.

In my case, I knew in advance that the acquisitions editor would be calling Penn on a particular Friday after the decision-making meeting of the review board. To keep myself from waiting by the phone, biting my nails to shreds, I purposely made a morning playdate for my daughter with a little boy whose mom I really liked. The plan was to dye Easter eggs with our toddlers—if anything was going to keep my mind temporarily off that imminent phone call, it was trying to keep two sets of greedy toddler hands out of blue and red dye.

That lovely spring Friday I was rewarded for my plan, and Penn called just as we were finishing with the eggs. In fact, I couldn't get to the phone right away, and had to call her back while my friend took the two kids into the playroom.

The news was good: Writer's Digest wanted to buy my book! Details would come early next week.

Celebrations ensued. Tentative toasts were enjoyed throughout the weekend on both coasts (my parents live out in California, and I live here on the East Coast). Tentative because nothing was official yet.

To make it official, I had a lot of paperwork to consider and negotiate with Penn. It took more than another month to sort all that out, which is not uncommon. The paperwork itself varies from deal to deal, so there is not much point in addressing those details here. Your agent will explain it all, and you should feel free to ask her all the questions you want about the document. When you do comb through your contract, do it with a clear head and a strong cup of coffee, since it'll be difficult to sort through all the legalese with that happy little voice in your head constantly whooping, "A book contract! A book contract!"

Ugh, why am I talking about paperwork when what you really want to know is *What comes next? Tell me all about how a book gets made!*

Next chapter, please.

PUBLISHED WRITING IS A *Team* EFFORT

*Y*ou know that image of Snoopy sitting on top of his house, pounding away at his typewriter, with only Woodstock as his occasional muse and helpmate? It's one of my favorite images of The Writer. Before I actually got published, it felt very close to the truth: Me and my computer, by ourselves, with thought bubbles above my head.

The first people I let into my process were a little like Woodstock—trusted friends who chirped away about my words. Over the years, though, I widened my circle of readers to include strangers, classmates, and teachers, and their ideas and opinions certainly shaped my work, but in essence it was still just me sitting and writing, like Snoopy. That was because before there was any promise of publication, the end products were only my drafts and revisions, which only I could produce.

Once an editor said yes to my first to-be-published short story, suddenly I wasn't the only one making decisions about the end product. I had to contend with a document full of comments in the margin, crossed-out words and phrases, inserted additions, and all manner of suggested changes. In my case, I was so overjoyed at the fact that I was going to be published at all that I didn't chafe at any of the requests. The editor's ideas jived nicely with mine, and I never felt like he was trying to make the piece into something it wasn't; I only felt that he was improving my story, taking what was already a seventh or eighth draft and making it *publishable*.

Which is exactly an editor's job: to see the potential in a piece of writing and feel a strong enough connection to it that he feels he can make it into a story or essay or poem worthy of the publication that bears his name. This is how I view my work at YARN, anyway, and it appears to be the attitude of all the editors I've worked with so far on my own writing. For short works published in magazines and journals, the writer and the editor become a small team, working together on the writing, which somehow becomes separate from the writer. At least, that has been my experience. Once something I've written has been selected for publication, it becomes a little less mine.

Some writers hate this teamwork. They complain bitterly about editors who don't understand their work or seem to be trying to change it unduly. Sometimes the writers are correct and the editors are overstepping their boundaries, and that is an opportunity to utilize your agent, who can help intervene if things seem to be going wrong. Sometimes, though, the problem is that the writer would prefer to be Snoopy on his roof, alone. The risk of overediting, or of somehow tainting a writer's style with editing, is insignificant compared to the risk of never getting published. I say if the editor likes your work and they make sense to you, trust his suggestions. And remember, you are a *team*. If some of the suggestions don't work for you, politely say so. I've had plenty of discussions with YARN writers about a change I've suggested, and I've been the one to back down in many cases, letting the writer have her way. Also remember that if one editor just isn't working for you, you don't have to work with him again. Take your next piece elsewhere!

For a short story or essay in a magazine or journal, the writer and editor are likely to be the only people on the publication team, though I once had a short story illustrated with beautiful drawings by a very talented artist. What a thrill it was to get my contributor's copies in the mail, open the magazine to my story, and see all the illustrations! A fantastic painter had been on my team, and I hadn't even known it.

The team dedicated to publishing a book, however, is much larger.

And yes, before you ask, I *will* discuss self-publishing, but after I wade through the weeds of traditional publishing. Even if you're almost positive you'll be going the self-publishing route with your own heartbreaking work of staggering genius, I suggest you read about traditional publishing as well since you'll have to go through just about all of the same steps anyway with a smaller team.

Book publishing starts with the writer and his agent, who probably made some editorial suggestions before sending the book to editors. Then the team grows to include the editor who makes the first set of suggestions for revisions to the manuscript. The editor might also have an assistant, a junior editor in training who does everything from fielding phone calls to starting the edit of the book (especially if it was the assistant who read the manuscript and first brought it to the attention of her boss).

The editorial process for a book works very much like it does for journal publishing, but more slowly because the team is working with a two- to four-hundred page beast instead of a five- to twenty-page pet. Fiction and nonfiction also have different processes. Fiction, especially your first novel, is sold based on a completed manuscript, so the editor can start his job right away. Nonfiction, however—like this book—is sold based on a proposal that contains a sample of about ten percent of the book, which means that the editor waits around for six months or more while the writer actually writes the book. For this book you're reading now, which is a fairly typical example, I had two due dates: one for the first half of the book and one for the whole book. At the midway point, my editor gave some suggestions, which helped me refine those first chapters and also shape the future chapters.

Once the writer makes the first set of changes based on the editor's comments, the book goes back to the editor for approval or another round of revisions. When the editor and writer agree that the book is ready, it goes to the copyeditor. Oh, copyeditors. They are those wonderfully detail-oriented people who are capable of finding all your niggling spelling, grammar, and sometimes factual errors (mostly, though, writers are responsible for getting their own facts straight). You want a good copyeditor, because without one, all your annoyed readers will be posting even more annoying typos on your Amazon review page. Readers *love* pointing out stuff like that. A strong copyedit is so important, I'd say, that if you get the sense that the copyeditor assigned to your book is less than stellar, I would seriously consider hiring a freelance copyeditor or employing your most grammatically inclined friend to give your book a close read.

While the copyediting is happening, other members of the book team will be coming out of the woodwork; in some cases, you'll have met these people already, but it's at this point that they start to become just as important as your editor. A designer will be assigned to work on the cover of your book and all the other aspects of its appearance (font, typeface, title page, and so on). The designer is likely to have a team of her own, who will work on different pieces of the design, not just for the hardcover or paperback that will be shelved at libraries and bookstores, but for the e-book that will be sold for Kindles, Nooks, and other e-readers.

Hopefully you'll get a cover like mine, which will surprise and delight you down to your toes. When my editor sent me a PDF of it one drizzly Thursday morning, I wasn't expecting it at all—wasn't expecting it to come so soon in the process, and wasn't expecting it to be so *cool*. From what I've heard, it's not always such a love fest, but since your agent is likely to have negotiated into your contract with the publisher that you have some input on the book's cover, you can expect to have some say. Just remember that the cover artist is just as serious about his craft as you are; if you have suggestions, lead with the positive.

Oh yes, and a photographer will take your author photo. You know, the picture that will be plastered all over the Internet as your book is heralded as the Next Big Thing. Yeah, that photo. Most writers I know have been in charge of getting their own author photo to the publisher, which means you can choose the photographer. Pull a few books down off your shelves, have a look at the head shots, and get a sense for what you want. Note especially how you *don't* want to look; give those pictures to your photographer and say, "Not this."

Around the same time, you'll also need to be thinking more and more about how you're going to make sure your image *does* get plastered all over the Internet. The publishing house will assign you a publicist, who likely comes with his own team as well, and they—along with your editor and your editor's boss, the publisher, who has always been on your team but might now start making more of an appearance—will be talking a lot about how to promote and position your book.

At this point, a lot of people would say I've covered everything about the team(s) working on the creation of your book. The book is the book; it's the object you can hold in your hands, whereas selling the book is a different matter. I disagree, because the way your book gets presented to the media and to readers is crucial to how people will imagine and receive your book. The quotes from established writers that appear on your back cover, the blurbs that go into advertising copy and publisher brochures—all of those things, and more, are just as important as the cover of your book and the quality of the copyediting. Sure, it's all window dressing, but who ever said window dressing wasn't important?

Alright, promotion. Don't plan on doing any writing for your next book while your other book is launching. During your book's crucial release time, promotion counts as writing in your planner. The amount of help a writer receives from the publisher in promoting a book varies widely and depends on many factors. Suffice it to say that even writers who receive lots of promotional help from the publisher often don't find it to be enough; they still have to do considerable work to make sure the book gets read. Also, all the expensive promotion in the world can't guarantee your book will get the one and only thing it needs in order to sell, sell, sell: word of mouth. People need to talk about your book, blog about it online, recommend it to friends and strangers on the bus, and be seen carrying it around campus.

How can you give your book the best shot at great and long-lasting word-of-mouth success? It starts with the blurb on the inside flap of your hardcover, or on the back cover if yours is a paperback original—those wildly flattering paragraphs that sum up your multi-layered book in ways that will likely horrify you and make you blush, simultaneously. You won't be writing that, because, well, how could you? You're too close to the book. I always thought my agent did a far better job of summarizing my books than I had, when I read the copy she wrote for the agency's website. *Really,* I thought, *I wrote that book?* You *will* help procure the quotes from famous writers that will appear all over your book's front and back covers, calling in every favor you're owed and making promises to repay new favors when you're in a position to do so. Be sure to get some nice stationery for your thank-you notes!

Once the book itself is in sell-worthy shape, it's all about advertising, reviews, and social media. Unless you're independently wealthy and can afford very expensive ads online and in newspapers, advertising is up to the publisher and what they are willing to spend to advertise your book. Brace yourself: Unless you are Suzanne Collins or potentially "the next Suzanne Collins," your book isn't likely to get a lot of advertising dollars.

The good news is, many important venues for promotion are free. While some media outlets charge money to push your book, most will write about you for free if they like your book. And no matter how much your publisher is spending on promotion, you will have the benefit of access to the house's sales and marketing people—their expertise in, and enthusiasm for, this part of the publication process (which, frankly, scares the bejeezus out of me) will be indispensable in planning and executing your promotion plan. Your editor and you, along with the sales and marketing teams, will work together to come up with a list of bloggers, reviewers, and print publications that might be interested in your book. Your publisher will reach out to some of these, and you'll have to reach out to others. Your author Facebook, Twitter, and Tumblr accounts are free. More and more, writers are launching books online instead of in a bookstore, with live chats, blog tours, and a Facebook and Twitter frenzy all designed to generate that precious word of mouth.

The promotion of a book is just as important as—if not *more* important than—writing a good book. So many beautiful books go nowhere because they were poorly promoted, and you know what happens to the writers of those books? They have a very hard time selling book number two, because the most important thing a publisher can hear about an already-published author's first book is that it "earned out." Earning out means that the book made back what the publisher paid for your advance, and that you've started to see some royalties. As a side note, if there is ever a time to be happy you got a tiny advance, it's when you're trying to earn out—an advance of $5,000 is way easier to earn back than an advance of $50,000, or $500,000 if you happen to be dreaming big. One blessing of a large advance, however, is that you might be able to afford to hire an independent literary publicist to do your promotion for you, if you can't bring yourself to get into it. The investment will pay dividends for your career down the line.

Speaking of advances, let's talk about self-publishing. You won't get an advance if you self-publish. In fact, you won't get any of the team members I detailed above if you self-publish, unless you hire them yourself. You *do*, however, have to take care of everything that would happen in a traditional publishing environment: You need to make sure your book is edited for content and properly copyedited by someone other than you; you need a cover design, promotional quotes, a promotion plan, and all that good stuff. It's a lot of work.

This isn't necessarily a bad thing. Having a team of one (you) means that although you'll need to work very hard, you don't have to share any of the profits if your book sells. True, you will need to make an initial investment in the editing and artistic design of your book— but hopefully you have some talented friends and family who will give you a great rate for their work (and hey, your thanks on your Acknowledgments page is a good promotional tool for their own arts). You will also have to swallow Amazon's (or Barnes and Noble's, or Apple's) standard profit-sharing rate for e-publishing, and if you plan to offer hardcopies of your book, you'll need to find a print-on-demand press with good rates and beautiful products that you might need to pay in advance. After you lay out those dollars, though, the money you make is yours. Just be sure you're prepared to get that word of mouth going.

It used to be that self-publishing was regarded as one-hundred percent vanity publishing, meaning that the supposedly vain writer in question, having been rejected from all the traditional publishing houses, wanted to thumb her nose at said publishing houses by self-publishing her book and making money anyway.

That's not the case anymore. Some writers—even established and famous writers—are deciding to circumvent traditional publishers and strike out on their own. While it's true that some writers turn to self-publishing after being rejected by traditional publishers, readers now respect the fact that many of those writers are excellent; they are not simply the vain and bitter rejects of the publishing industry. As you know if you've read at least some of the earlier chapters of this book, writers get rejected for many reasons, and quality is only one reason among many. Recognizing this change in the industry, awards by prestigious institutions have sprung up to honor excellence in self-publishing.

It's a course to consider, for sure. As I hope I advised strongly enough earlier, though, no writer should cut corners if he hopes for his book to be recognized in the field of self-publishing. There is a lot of poorly written, unedited *crap* out there. If you want to be a successful writer-preneur, do it right and make yourself into a one-(wo)man publishing house. And best of luck to you! Seriously.

In the end, we *all* need luck in publishing. No matter how many people are on your team, once that book hits the stores, everyone is crossing their fingers. Publishing is full of stories that expose this dark truth: Except in a handful of cases, no one really knows when books are going to take off like wildfire. The Harry Potter series was a sleeper hit, as was *Cold Mountain, Divine Secrets of the Ya-Ya Sisterhood*, and many others.

I suppose we should find that comforting. It means that if our books don't make it onto the bestseller lists, we're in good company. It means that success could happen with any book. It means that we're all in this thing together; we're all on the same team.

READERS ARE THE *Best Friends* A *Writer* WILL NEVER MEET*

One of my favorite passages in literature is from Italo Calvino's *If on a winter's night a traveler*—in it, the narrator stands in the bookstore listing all the different kinds of books every true reader wants and owns but will likely never read, including "Books That Everybody's Read So It's As If You Had Read Them, Too," "Books You Want To Own So They'll Be Handy Just In Case," and "Books You Need To Go With Other Books On Your Shelves." Somehow this passage has always captured the disconnect between the reality and fiction of my own reading life.

Also, I've never been a big poetry person, and I'm jealous of people who actually enjoy Joseph Conrad and Graham Greene—do they have a critical literary gene that I'm missing? Now that I am out of school, if given the choice between curling up with *Heart of Darkness* (which, for the record, I've read three times) and curling up with the new issue of *Bon Appetit*, the latter would win every time.

---

*An earlier version of this essay, entitled "Confessions of a Dangerous Reader and Teacher," appeared in the *Poets and Writers* digital edition (http://www.pw.org/content/confessions_dangerous_reader_and_teacher?cmnt_all=1).

I think Netflix is the best invention ever.

I own a TV and I'm not afraid to use it.

I go to the gym.

And that's only the beginning ...

So at the end of this book about the sanctity of writing, I must confess that I don't always put my money where my mouth is, literature-wise. I give in to temptations of all sorts when it comes to divvying up my free time. To justify my weak will, I've often argued things like, "Plenty of movies and TV shows (*Mad Men, The Kids Are All Right*) teach me about storytelling as well as written stories." But the fact is that many of the movies I find myself watching (*The Hangover Part II*) don't offer a lot of instruction; instead, they're good for facilitating my escape from the real world.

Engaging in activities like movie watching and magazine flipping gives me that fabulous sensation of quick-fix deliverance from my daily cares (which include writing). I can think shallow, easy thoughts, like: *Mike and I could take Elena on that vacation.* Or, *chili pepper flakes would liven up this sauce a lot.* Or, *at least I'm not as shallow as the heroine of this movie.* By comparison, sitting down to read a good book feels like too much of an investment.

Overworked modern people feel entitled to such fixes. We think, *I've got so much to do!* Why take the time to (re-)read a classic like *The Lion, the Witch, and the Wardrobe* when we can rent the DVD, offering us the chance to kill two birds (experiencing the story and still finishing our homework) with one stone?

While it's true that I'm as much a victim of this quick-fix mentality as the next person, I still love to read. And when I do take the time to sit down with a good book, it feels like a luxury. When I abandon myself to it, I can feel my very soul expanding.

I am not alone in my unfortunate ability to marginalize book reading in my daily schedule. In 2004, the National Endowment for the Arts published a seminal study on the reading habits of Americans called *Reading at Risk*, which indicated that fewer of us are reading these days than ever before. Fewer of us are seeking that soul expansion that die-hard readers crave on a regular basis. At the time it came out, there was a major outcry in the literary community, bemoaning this seemingly permanent loss of readers. While there have always been critics of the NEA's report, especially for its perhaps too-narrow definition of reading, and more recent studies have actually noted an uptick in Americans' overall reading habits, sales of actual *books* still flounder, and publishers are scrambling around trying to figure out how to capture new readers in this digital age.

This is bad news for writers. Without readers, who are we writing for? Books are a business just like any other. Books need to sell in order to survive. This is not a radical thought, but it is one that doesn't occur to a surprising number of writers. It certainly didn't occur to me in a personal, visceral way until I was much older, when I joined a group of professors in trying to draft a literacy program at the university where I taught. The group was formed in response to the low—and falling—circulation numbers in the university's library. We huddled together for the first time on a bleak February day in the warmth of the library's multimedia room, shutting ourselves in from the cold outside.

Before we started talking, we each filled out a short questionnaire about our own reading habits that included questions such as *Do you mainly read for: a) pleasure, b) current events, or c) research;* and *How many novels have you read in the last six months: a) less than 5, b) 5–15, or c) more than 15.* That was when I realized—and I said so at the meeting to an abbreviated chorus of similarly embarrassed laughs—that, looking at my answers, I might actually be part of the problem we were trying to fix.

At dinner that night, I was telling Mike about our meeting, and he said, "Sounds like you're trying to ensure a market for your work."

I thought this was unbelievably demeaning. I, a writer—*an artiste!*—was not going to be lowered to the bottom-line demands of the marketplace, to filthy lucre. Ensure a market, indeed. As a professor, I aspired to something much loftier: to shaping my students' malleable minds with great words and ideas, to inspiring in them a hunger for knowledge, a desire to spurn the market-driven mentality of the Internet and television. As a writer, I aspired to entertain as well as to teach, to make my readers think about the world in new and challenging ways.

Realizing that I'd taken offense to his suggestion, Mike took a moment to clarify: "Don't get me wrong—I think you *should* be trying to ensure a market base for your product." My product being the future novels that would hopefully fly off Amazon's virtual bookshelves.

He was, in short, encouraging me to do the very thing all book people need to do: stop—and, if possible, reverse—the erosion of our market base. Reading is as much at the mercy of the marketplace as Facebook stock. And because book reading is just one of many priorities for everyone these days, the commodity associated with the activity will get purchased only if that activity is at the top of a person's list of priorities. However much we wish this weren't the case, writers are competing for the time, attention, and dollars of potential readers.

I'm not going to candy-coat it: We writers have an obligation to our own writing and to writing as an art and industry, to pitch in and help figure out how to motivate people to read more. Readers truly are the best friends a writer will never meet.

I suspect that at this point many of you are shifting nervously in your seats. It's easy for writers to get drunk on a strong denial of the realities of the marketplace (*Look at James Joyce; he was broke his entire career!*), and so our world is full of an insidious prejudice against writers who have embraced those realities. They and their ideas are considered dangerous. Editors and publicists, with whom many writers plead to do all the promotional work, know the truth. Of course, some writers embrace the market. Many writers self-publish and self-promote. Others network constantly in person and online. What I'm suggesting—a writer-led, nationwide grassroots "Back to Books!" campaign—is another of these market-embracing tactics, but with broader goals than a book deal. Think of it as enlightened self-interest.

In an earlier version of this essay, I argued that teachers are in an ideal position to "market" books to their students because writer-teachers see their students every week, and they have the attention of those students for three months or a year of their formative intellectual years. For the months teachers hold sway over their students, teaching them to read and write, the students belong to the very community of writers to which the writer-teachers themselves belong. It's really pretty exciting.

But you're probably not yet a teacher, so you need different advice on how to bring people back to books. It's never too early to start thinking about this critically important aspect of the writing life. Also, I have a dream that if this book reaches the hands of enough aspiring young writers, you guys might be able to tip the balance in your generation in favor of books.

I can't possibly list, let alone think of, all the possible ways we can make books more popular, but I can share some of the great ideas I've seen implemented by people I admire. Some are very simple and others require more effort, but all of them should get your wheels turning on this incredibly important topic:

- Go to readings of authors that sound interesting at your local library and bookstores. Bring friends.
- Volunteer at, apply to work at, or (at a minimum) attend a nearby book fair. Terra Elan McVoy, a YA novelist, is the program director for the AJC Decatur Book Festival, meaning she curates and oversees all the events for the festival. This struck me as a wonderful occupation for a writer—not only does it allow her to immerse herself in books she loves, her efforts help spur the sales of books. If you happen to be an older reader of this book, you might even consider founding your very own local book fair. No matter what your age, when you go, be sure to bring friends.
- Start a book group. Open it up to anyone at your school or in your dorm. You never know who might show up.
- Start or volunteer for a literacy organization, especially in neighborhoods where reading is typically undervalued. I'm always amazed and impressed by what I see in the news about industrious teens like Lilly Leight, who's working hard to promote reading in her community through a multilayered "read-

ing ecosystem" that won her an Innovations in Reading Prize from the National Book Foundation.

- Along those same lines, you could spearhead an effort to raise money at your school for books to replace those lost at libraries and schools in natural disasters like Hurricane Katrina.
- Start a blog about books, authors, or anything reading related that you love. Essentially, that's what my literary journal YARN is: a website for YA writing, which I love.
- Tweet more to your family and friends about books you like, or even those you hate. It really is true that bad publicity is better than no publicity.
- Suggest reading dates. Sounds geeky, but sometimes nothing is sexier than hanging out on a couch, legs intertwined, with two cups of hot chocolate and two books (and yes, comics count!).
- Participate in discussions, in person and online, where you have the opportunity to promote books. The summer I was writing this book, NPR sponsored a list of "100 Best-Ever Teen Novels," and YARN answered with its own Blockbuster-Free Summer Reading Exchange. Both were opportunities to recommend books you love and talk about them with others. YARN's exchange was also a way to highlight books that don't get enough attention in the media, and other websites host similar discussions. One humble piece of advice: When you are engaged with other readers, think of it not as an opportunity to congratulate Major Writers once again, but to break in and say, "Have you heard of This Fabulous Writer Not Enough People Are Reading Yet?"

I'll be right there with you, in the trenches, bringing as many people back to books as I can—through YARN, through my writing, and through the rest of my career, whatever it may bring. Also, since I had that little epiphany about what a terrible reader I was becoming, I've tried my best to reverse the damage, and I try to make time for reading books whenever I can. Yes, even if that means turning off the television.

You might be the kind of writer you perceive me to be, an aspiring novelist who also loves editing, teaching writing, and writing nonfiction, but I hope that many other kinds of writers are reading these words as well: Emily Dickinsons who might publish only a tiny fraction of their oeuvre during their lifetimes, future editors, lawyers, academics who decided they didn't want to write the next great American novel after all, and maybe even the next Suzanne Collins or J.K. Rowling.

What unites all of us, I hope, is that we are rooting for words: novels, biographies, poetry, journals, plays, short stories, essays—you name it. I very much want our publication dreams to come true, but even more, I want us to keep in mind that the writing life is long and rewarding in many ways, and that reading, the pleasure we take in words that are not our own, will be with us all the while.

Appendix

(NOT THE ONE YOU HAD OUT WHEN YOU WERE 10)*

*I*f you followed me here from "Sorry, But Yes, You Do Have to 'Get a Real Job,'" I'm glad. Shannon wisely pointed out that many readers would be interested in this list because they already have no intention of making creative writing their profession, but they still want to work with words in a creative way. Others of you might just be looking for ways to support your writing habit. Please keep in mind as you (and your parents—*Hi, parents!*) read this chapter that this is not meant to be a comprehensive list of professions for a writer; rather, it's a personal list culled from the writers I've known and kept in touch with since high school.

Also, here are three notes about *all* of the professions listed below, so I don't have to repeat myself a million times. One: Not only will these jobs pay you, they will provide you with the kinds of experiences that will fill your creative writing with authentic,

---

*We don't want you to miss out on more jobs you might be interested in, like being a librarian, speech writer, nanny, parent, temp, or retailer. To find out more about those, head over to www.writersdigest.com/this-is-not-a-writing-manual.

unique details. If it makes working for money more palatable, think of your job as research; every day you go to your desk, you're gathering material for your novel. And remember that T.S. Eliot was, by turns, a teacher, a banker, and an editor by day. Two: Many of the word-oriented jobs below can also make you a faster, more flexible writer and editor of your own work—I mean, if you're dealing with words all day, you will naturally get better at dealing with words in general. Three: The trick with selecting any paid profession is to choose one that won't kill your creative writing if indeed you plan to work on your creative writing in your spare time. Some of the jobs below might wind up replacing your creative writing, and you might be pleasantly surprised to find that you don't care—that in fact, you *prefer* writing advertising copy to writing short stories. If, however, you discover that you really like editing but find that you don't even want to look at another novel when you get home at the end of the day … well, it's probably time to try something else that won't kill your creative writing.

The good news? You're young! Internships and entry-level positions in any industry will provide you with transferable skills that can help you get a job in a different industry if you decide to switch (well, maybe going from editing to rocket science would be a hard sell for an employer, but going from editing to public relations shouldn't be too difficult). And even if you're older, keep in mind that nothing is set in stone. You are always in charge of your own life, and you always have time to make a change.

Journalism and Reviewing

Yes, you can actually get paid for your writing! Though newspapers are cutting back staff and trying to figure out their business models for the future, you can enter a whole world of paying print and online magazines. Here's a short list of publications my aspiring-writer friends and novelist-teachers have been paid to write for:

- *Details* and *GQ* (Both of these glossies are men's lifestyle magazines with fashion, trends, and articles about everything from movies to marriage.)

- *Publishers Weekly* and *Booklist* (These are two of the most highly respected review magazines in publishing; when a writer gets a good review in one of these, it's always featured on the book's promotional materials.)
- *The Washington Post* and *The New York Times* (As I'm sure you know, these two newspapers are the leaders in breaking news and analysis for local, national, and international news.)
- *NYLON* and *NYLON Guys* (These brother-sister glossies offer articles on cutting-edge fashion, travel, music, and other trends.)
- *Rolling Stone* (The music industry's leading magazine, covering everything from Taylor Swift to indie bands.)
- *The New Yorker* (Since 1925, it's been the weekly source for the best in fiction, commentary, satire, and poetry. The cartoons alone are an artistic education.)
- *True/Slant* (Trueslant.com is an online destination for well-crafted blogs and social media on almost every subject—film, politics, science, parenting, and money.)
- *Slate* (In its own words, this is an "online magazine of news, politics, and culture." My friends always seem to be sharing links from *Slate* on Facebook.)
- *Elle* (It's like *Vogue*, but more irreverent.)

The more well known the publication, the better the pay, but, of course, the harder it is to write for. Just to give you an idea, a weekly local entertainment and reviews magazine pays close to $0.30 per word, and Condé Nast publications like *Vogue* pay closer to $4 per word for articles of varying lengths (250 words to 5,000 words or longer). Most publications like to hire freelance writers, contracting them for a certain number of words per article, month, or year, which helps them cut their costs, but ambitious freelance writers can still cobble together a decent living. Though you might not be on the masthead, you'll be listed as a contributing writer, and you'll be building a portfolio of clips that will help you get better and better assignments.

It starts with being willing to write for unglamorous publications that pay very little. Jonny Segura, a friend from my MFA program and a published novelist, started out as a beat reporter in Omaha, Nebraska, and was later a reviews editor at *Publishers Weekly*. Another friend, Kristin Hussey, got her start with two internships at big city papers, one at *The Washington Times* and the other at the *Los Angeles Times*, before getting her career started as a full-time general assignment reporter at a decidedly smaller paper, *The News* of Boca Raton, Florida. Her own college mentor told her that while everyone wants to start at *The New York Times*, "you'll have *a lot* more fun and get more experience at a small local paper," and she says her own experience proved that to be absolutely true—and I can add that when she tells stories about those days in Boca Raton, everyone is riveted. Still, fewer than two years later she moved on to *The Capital* of Annapolis, Maryland, and then to *The Wall Street Journal Online*, despite her confession at the job interview that she knew, in her words, "virtually nothing about finance or Wall Street," because what mattered to the editor who hired her was that she was a smart, experienced writer who could learn the finance side. As she said, "The great thing about journalism is you get to learn about everything under the sun."

It's important to be flexible and humble at the start. If they ask you to cover the police blotter but you'd rather review films or books, take the job they're offering. Get your foot in the door and work your way up. It's an old-fashioned trajectory, but it still works. And don't forget about the vast array of opportunities in the blogosphere. You might not get paid for launching your own blog or doing a weekly column for a friend's blog, but you will improve your craft, build publication credits, and maybe even gain some industry attention. A personal blog is something that editors at other publications can look at to get a sense of your writing ability and dedication. It can also help you find an audience and lead you to unexpected opportunities. Teen writer Tavi Gevinson is a great example; she started her own style blog and was able to grow it into an online publication (http://rookiemag.com/us) endorsed by big media types like Ira Glass of *This American Life*.

Most of the professors I had in the MFA program at Columbia—and indeed, the professors at most MFAs across the country—write articles and book reviews in addition to teaching and writing their novels and poetry. These are writers at the absolute top of their games, writers whose books are featured in *The New York Times Book Review* and sometimes make it onto the bestseller lists. They write articles and book reviews to make ends meet, true, but also because it makes them more visible public figures. Some of the most prominent novelists in American and English letters—Henry James, Virginia Woolf, John Dos Passos—contributed to the intellectual history of ideas with their fiction *and* their reviews and journalism. It's no different today, but the good news is that with the advent of the Internet, there are many more places to publish that kind of work.

Which doesn't mean you have to be publishing "important" writing in order to make money. If you'd rather write a sex column for *Nerve* or *Cosmo*, go for it. Hey, it worked for Candace Bushnell.

Become an Editor or an Agent

Like journalism and reviewing, editing and agenting are directly related to your creative writing—perhaps more so. In fact, if I have any criticism of these careers for the aspiring writer, it's that they are so closely related to what you want to be that you might find them a tad depressing. When I interned for an agent after college, I found the sheer volume of *talent* out there competing for publication and readership disheartening at times. The trick, I discovered, is to figure out where you fit in publishing and make it work for you; I learned that I fit in better at YARN than I did in an agent's office.

After all, the publishing industry does promote its own—look at David Levithan, a massively successful editor at Scholastic *and* novelist in his own right. Dawn Raffel, a noted writer of avant-garde fiction, also made a strong career on the editing staff of magazines like *O, The Oprah Magazine*. On a smaller scale, I have noticed that my friends who founded respected literary journals have had an easier time getting their writing published *after* becoming editors. Publishing is like any industry: You've got to get your foot in the door somehow.

It may turn out that you prefer editing or agenting the work of others to actually writing your own. More than one acquaintance from my MFA years took internships with agents and editors while they were students and *loved* the work. They realized as they read the slush and helped make sales that they were really cut out to shepherd writers through the process of making novels or bringing articles to press. As my own agent Penn puts it on her bio for the Ann Rittenberg Literary Agency, "After discovering that my B.A. in poetry writing from the University of Virginia didn't exactly flood my mailbox with job offers, I moved to New York to pursue a career in publishing."

Like many college grads considering a career on the other side of publishing, Penn attended the New York University Summer Publishing Institute. Since my first post-college roommate also attended a program like it, I happen to know that these programs, especially those in New York, are hotbeds of ambition, filled with word-loving folks who form lifelong friendships and professional alliances while working hard and having loads of fun in the city. If you do want to get a job in the New York publishing industry, you might consider going to one of these programs, particularly since they are also famous for helping their students get paying jobs at top-notch publishing houses and magazines.

Editing can also take many forms, way beyond the obvious career in a trade publishing house, for which you start as a poorly paid but respectable editorial assistant, then work your way up to assistant editor, then editor, and maybe even senior editor or publisher someday if you do really well. You can also follow my path and that of some of my friends and launch your own literary journal—but this likely won't pay you. Or you can make like my playwright friend and get a job writing and editing in-house publications and press releases at a large corporation, and get paid very well indeed. Or you can get an editing gig at a medical journal, particularly if you have some knowledge of science— or any other kind of niche magazine or journal for that matter. If you know about fly-fishing or muscle cars or cakes, look into magazines and journals that feature your specialty. Again, you'll likely start as an assistant or a copyeditor and work your way up from there. Your college might even have a university press that is looking for a junior editor— apply for that job, too! I once spent a blissful summer at UCLA factchecking and editing the manuscript of an English professor whose book involved some math, which had scared away the grad students to whom he'd spoken about the job. I'm no expert in math, but all my relevant geometry and algebra came back to me with the help of the Internet, and later on, he paid me to do the index for the same book.

Editing jobs outside the world of New York trade houses—the ones that publish the books you probably want to write—have several virtues. For one, the job might not be in New York City, which saves you the horror of finding affordable city housing and the expense of actually living in one of the five boroughs. For another, you won't have to face the slush pile every day, which means you won't be thinking to yourself every morning, "One day, *my* novel is going to be in that pile," a thought that is likely to make you want to vomit up your five dollar latte one fine morning.

Copywriting and Ghostwriting

Like journalism, agenting, and editing, copywriting and ghostwriting can get your foot in the door. Plus, it can help you hone your craft— these jobs require you to adopt a voice that's not your own and use it consistently throughout, which is no easy task. In a perhaps controversial move, I've put these two types of writing together because for both, your name as the writer isn't particularly important. In the case of ghostwriting, you're literally writing as someone else—a celebrity, perhaps, or a romance novelist who can't write enough on her own and needs help to produce those ten paperbacks a year in her name. This kind of writing job is also much, much harder to get than copywriting.

You might get paid close to twenty grand to ghostwrite a For Dummies book, which would have seemed like a lot of money to my eighteen-year-old self for six months of work, but by the time I was twenty-eight, I realized that in order to live in New York, I'd have to make at least three times that, and even then I wouldn't be able to save for a house or retirement. But! If you make a name for yourself as a ghostwriter, you can start making closer to one hundred grand for a project. Not bad. And you can do it in your pajamas.

Copywriting happens in so many different contexts, it's hard to account for them all. Like the niche editing I discussed before, copywriting is necessary for many magazines and journals, as well as big companies, universities, hospitals, and other corporations that produce newsletters, memos, signs, and literally all the written material you see, say, when you go to your doctor's office. Someone is writing all that stuff, and getting paid to do it—maybe it should be you, especially if you're the kind of person who hates to see misplaced apostrophes. Sometimes the job of "copywriter" involves some editing as well, or leads to an editing job in the company.

This work isn't always called copywriting anymore. When you plug your search terms into a job listings website, you'll want to use that creative mind of yours and try phrases like "internal marketing," "content creator," "technical writer," or "producer of content," because those are the words that describe copywriting jobs these days. A lot of writing is generated just for the employees of a company, or "in-house," which needs copywriters. But copywriting also happens in my next category, which includes PR (public relations) and advertising—that's writing meant for the world outside of the company.

PR, Advertising, and Social Media Networking

These professions make the media machine run. I grouped them together because they are so often grouped together in panel discussions and at company meetings, and because they are all jobs that *promote* stuff, whether that stuff is books, museums, aspirin, diapers, or celebrities. Unlike the copywriting and editing that happens for the employees of a company, this writing and editing happens for all of us.

When I was young, I was confused for a long time about the difference between PR and advertising. It turns out that advertising is much more straightforward than PR. When we see an ad on TV, the Internet, or in a magazine, we recognize it instantly. It's trying to sell us something. Someone at that cat food company was in charge of creating that ad and getting it in front of us. Sometimes the making of the ad happens in-house, which means there's a team of people at the cat food company who come up with the words and images that constitute the ad, and another team of people in charge of selling that ad to magazines and other media outlets. The cat food company may also hire an advertising agency that specializes in making cool ads, à la *Mad Men*.

Typically, aspiring writers like to be on the "creative" side of advertising, which means they want to be the trend makers coming up with the concepts and words that appear in the ad itself. From what I've heard, those jobs pay pretty well. You might want to keep in mind the following anecdote, though: YARN's first poetry editor, Colleen Oakley, has a friend who does ads for a big-name liquor company. When Colleen's husband observed, "That sounds fun," the ad guy replied that advertising has changed in the last decade. It's not as creative as when he got into it. It's all data now. Analytics. Statistics. As Colleen punctuated the story, "The future of advertising, baby, is *data*."

The same is true for PR, which is a far larger and more complicated category of work. Nebulously named "public relations," it really does cover all the work that's done to communicate between a company and the public, and jobs in this industry might also be called marketing, communications, and/or content jobs. Let's look at the cat food company again. The company wants to make sure its product is featured in magazine articles, not just in ad form. You know those "editor's choice" pages in magazines, where the editors tell you all about the products they love? In many cases, they found out about the product because a PR person from the company sent them a fun package of swag featuring the product—cat food—as well as all the written information on why their cat food is *the best* cat food. A team of people create that package to send out, and it includes writing. Someone's got to do that writing!

What if the cat food had to be recalled? Salmonella was discovered in the salmon. A team of PR people also does the damage control for that recall, issuing written press releases to the media and preparing speeches and memos for the CEO to send out as necessary. Or what if the cat food company is releasing a new vegan cat food? The PR team is in charge of getting the word, or "content," out.

Both advertising and PR can happen in-house, but sometimes a company will hire an outside creative agency to handle various promotional items and activities. My friend Mike Harvkey, a writer I met during my MFA years who is also a gifted visual artist, contracted himself out to just such an agency to write and conceptualize promotional campaigns at a rate of $450 a day, for places like Nickelodeon and Nick Jr., the Sundance Channel, and the Discovery Channel. In this industry, you can start as an assistant or freelancer, but mainly you work your way up by building a set of clips. Unlike in journalism, for which your clips need to be published, you can create a portfolio of clips from classes you've taken or ideas you've storyboarded in your free time.

If you think you might be interesting in advertising or PR and you're looking for something to do one summer, you might want to consider classes at your local community college in statistics, web design, HTML, and graphic design. One friend who works in marketing for a big company says that most "content" jobs, even for financial and law firms, ask writers to multitask. On her last job search, she saw loads of job descriptions for PR and marketing positions that required at least basic graphic design skills to format e-mail blasts, blogs, and newsletters. You never know when those skills will come in handy.

I'm saving social networking for last because it's a relatively new career to pursue, and these days the person in charge of social networking often has other duties. It's usually housed with PR since broadcasting company news via Facebook and Twitter and reaching out to bloggers are acts of public relations. You know when you "like" a company on Facebook (a publishing house, a rock band, your favorite cat food brand) and then receive updates about sales, concerts, and other newsy tidbits related to the company? Well, someone is getting paid to write those updates. Sometimes, the social networking campaigns of your favorite (usually, shall we say, *older*) writers are being led by some industrious young writer behind the scenes.

Maybe it should be you.

The Law

It worked for John Grisham, right?

Personal Assistant

Before I started grad school, I worked as a personal assistant (PA) for a Famous Writer. Basically, I was required to show up at her apartment on a set schedule and perform a variety of tasks she didn't have time to perform herself, like packing all of her books for her move, organizing decades worth of her published writing, making a phone call here and there, and fetching muffins and iced coffee—for both of us, I might add. When I took the job, I thought I'd learn so much about being a writer and make so many connections! Not so in my case. Though we got along quite well when I worked for her and we parted on good terms, we're no longer in touch.

I know people, though, whose PA jobs got them invited to big parties and paid them quite a lot of money. Some of them had to sign nondisclosure agreements and couldn't actually tell anyone the name of the person they were working for. Sometimes those jobs were more specific than the general PA work I described above, as they were doing a particular project like cataloguing a family's art collection. Even when the PA job paid well, and came with reasonable hours, I have to say that usually the workers complained about them. It's difficult to work for a family or a single person; it can be very claustrophobic. On the upside, however, they do provide a young writer with plenty of material for characters in a novel!

Nonprofit Organizations (NPOs), Especially Those for Reading and Writing

When I joined Facebook a few years after finishing my MFA, I reconnected with a bunch of grad school friends and noted what interesting careers they had embarked upon. Some were the reviewers and journalists and copywriters I've already described, but two of them were directors at nonprofit writing centers for kids.

A few clicks of the mouse showed me what amazing jobs these are. My friends and their colleagues ran fantastic programs for children and teens—tutoring, writing workshops, publishing internships, and more. Maybe you attend one of these places already and can vouch for their excellence. Writing centers of this sort are popping up all over the country: Writopia is in New York, DC, and LA; the 826 Valencia Street center started in San Francisco and opened outposts across the country; and a host of other independent centers have also opened, like the Richard Hugo House in Seattle, Washington, and The Telling Room in Portland, Maine. Try Googling "writing center" in your neck of the woods, or ask at your local library. One might already exist near you.

When you graduate from college, consider working at one of these centers. True, many of the staff people are volunteers, but volunteering to tutor a few nights a week could lead to a paid job. A host of other kinds of arts NPOs are looking for smart, young, arts-minded types, too. One friend from grad school worked for a ballet company in New York, and another worked for the opera. At a lunch I attended recently, I met some very cool people who run a literacy program for incarcerated youth.

Getting to the top of one of these NPOs usually requires a master's degree in either writing or nonprofit organization management, but not always. And even if you can't have The Job right after college, it's the kind of career to keep in mind as you ponder "the rest of your life," particularly since these kinds of organizations attract so many writers (as founders, on their boards, as volunteers, as guest teachers, and as fundraisers) and thus can be a great way to meet other writers locally and nationally. If you *are* planning to publish a novel someday, you'll need all the connections you can gather!

Grant Writing and Other Fundraising

Those NPOs I was just talking about? They stay afloat with grant money and private donations. Guess how those grants are secured? Written applications. And private donations are secured through letter-writing campaigns. Someone has to write all that stuff!

Truly, becoming an experienced grant writer is a boon for any writer. Arts, media, and science organizations are *always* looking for more money, and they need savvy writers to help get it. As a bonus: It's great practice for when you apply for your own NEA grant to support your third novel. You know, the one that requires you to live in Paris for two months and eat pastries ... err, I mean, research the French Revolution.

And grants and letters aren't the only way that organizations raise money. They throw big parties, host readings and lectures, and constantly reach out to other like-minded individuals, foundations, and organizations to dream up new ways to raise the money. In essence, this is another kind of PR job. At tiny literacy organizations like the ones I mentioned in the last section, employees must wear many hats—teacher, marketer, grants researcher—which give them fantastic job experiences that can also be artistically fulfilling. At larger organizations, your job might be more specific, but you'll collaborate with people doing other jobs that might also interest you.

When you're in college, you could get a jump-start on this career track by looking for summer and work-study positions in your college development office, where you might write grants or thank-you letters, or even go out and visit donors and have fancy meals (on someone else's dime). You could also intern as an events planner or help out with an NPO's annual gala fundraiser or your local city's or college's summer arts festival. Another friend of Colleen's made good money assisting a for-profit corporate events planner and parlayed that experience to become an events coordinator and booker at major New York theaters. Even though grant writing and fundraising don't sound like particularly sexy work, you can use that early experience to get a job on the party side of the fundraising equation, where you'll meet all kinds of fun and important people.

Be an Entrepreneur

When YARN won an Innovations in Reading Prize from the National Book Foundation, we were completely humbled to be in the company of the other literary organizations who also won the prize. Some of the organizations that won, both that year and in the past, actually made money and employed people. One of these, Electric Literature, was the first to launch a top-notch literary journal on the iPhone and iPad, and now they run a fiction magazine called *Recommended Reading*, which features one piece of fiction per week and is curated by a well-known editor or writer.

The National Book Foundation honors many other reading- and writing-related projects, and the list of prize winners might give you some good ideas for projects you could start in your own hometown. Founding a company or a literary magazine can get you noticed in your local community and beyond. Running it puts you very much in charge of your own life. And if you pick a project in the literary arts, you'll be surrounded every day by the words and writers you love most. Not a bad way to pass the time.

You have to know the pros and cons, however. YARN is a lot like Electric Literature—we're both literary journals after all. YARN was the first independent literary journal to publish YA by writers of all ages online, and Electric Literature was the first to publish a literary journal with the best literary fiction writers on the iPad. But their initial goals were loftier than ours—they set out to build a business from their reading community. We set out to build the community, and now we're trying to figure out the business model. The bottom line is that because we followed an older, more altruistic model for our journal, YARN isn't bringing in any money yet; EL is. Think about these things before you get going.

Self-styled, freelance literary entrepreneurs who promote books and writers in this new and shifting publishing world are also on the rise. They might get hired by publishers or by the writers themselves, and they do all kinds of things from soliciting reviews and interviews to producing podcasts and book trailers.

Frankly, the world *needs* more literary entrepreneurs who are going to rethink the book business in the digital age. Writers—all of them, not just you and me—need people who are thinking smartly and very much outside the box about how to get writers noticed by a community of readers who download books at the click of a button instead of buying them from their local bookstores or reading them on the recommendation of their local libraries. The industry also needs people who think about how to get people reading *at all*, instead of playing tennis on their Wii. It needs people who think about new kinds of contracts that fairly compensate writers and charge readers for books that are available both on shelves and online.

Maybe that should be you.

Stray Thoughts:
Interning, Part Time vs. Full Time, Health Insurance, and Charging What You're Worth

When I sent out this chapter to friends of mine who actually do some of the jobs I've talked about, they helped me by performing some great fact-checking, and they also mentioned some good advice that I feel obligated to pass along here.

In this Appendix and other chapters in this book, I've mentioned interning as a way to get your foot in the door and gain some work experience, even if it's not in the field you wind up in. For instance, my internship at the Guggenheim Museum was impressive to employers in New York City for several years after I graduated college, even though I wasn't applying for art-related jobs. Internships tend to be worth your (usually) free labor, if you can afford to donate it.

The question of full time versus part time is a big one, especially for writers who want to work on their novel/screenplay/whatever on the side. My writer friends and I—and my nonwriter husband for what it's worth—have all done both, mixing up a few part-time gigs to make ends meet sometimes, and getting salaried full-time work at other times. Often, the choice was dictated by factors outside of our control: When the economy was in the toilet and full-time work was scarce, it was easier to piece together multiple part-time jobs. For some, piecemeal work resulted in better overall pay than did salaried jobs. I suspect that in your lifetime you'll likely do both for economic and other unpredictable reasons. I'm not convinced one is better than the other, though one thing I can say about the freelance life is that it takes some hustle, and juggling multiple jobs can get tiring. It also isn't likely to provide you with health insurance.

Which brings me to that very important subject. The bad news is that employers like to hire part-time workers because they aren't required to offer them health care and other goodies like retirement plans. The good news is that with the advent of Obamacare, you'll be eligible to stay on your parents' health insurance until you're twenty-six, which was something I was able to do way back in the 1990s, as my mother was a public school teacher and her insurance allowed for this perk. This means that you can have multiple part-time jobs without worrying about getting your own health insurance plan until about five years after you finish college. Then—or before then, if your parents don't have a good enough plan for you—you'll have to start making some decisions about jobs that may or may not include a plan, or what kind of plan to purchase with the freelance money you're making. Also keep in mind that your health isn't the only thing you should be thinking about; though you're young, it's never too early to start thinking about retirement. I know, I know, it's a drag—and it seems so far away. At some point, though, you'll need to start squirreling money away into your own retirement account. You might need to consider a job that offers a 401(k) plan.

By the time you start thinking about that retirement plan, you'll have gotten enough job experience and expertise to start charging real money for your services, whether it's ghostwriting or freelance editing. I'm going to quote my friend who has worked all over the publishing industry, because her e-mail to me said it better than I ever could: "I think one thing you might include in your book is something about negotiation. Business people don't think twice about charging $100 an hour (or much, much more) for their time, but writers, even good writers, consistently undervalue their services. They sell themselves short and lowball the prices they charge for services." Don't do that! I almost keeled over with surprise and something close to embarrassment when Mike suggested I charge $100 an hour for my tutoring services, but guess what? I got it. And there are plenty of people out there charging even more.

All of which is to say, *believe in yourself.* Believe in yourself as a writer, wherever that identity takes you.

BIBLIOGRAPHY

This is not meant to be a comprehensive or canonical list of books on writing. Rather, it's a very personalized list of books I have read and respect, or that close writer friends have read and respect (at a minimum, I have skimmed, read an excerpt, or heard the writer read from each of the works). Note, too, that I am a very slow and meticulous reader, which means that I simply haven't gotten to all the important books on writing that do exist; please don't hold any gaping holes in my repertoire against me.

I've also divided this list into categories instead of annotating the whole bibliography, to give you some sense of what the books are about. Although some of them could appear in multiple categories, I've tried my best to place each into the category that fits most of the book.

On Grammar

Fish, Stanley Eugene. *How to Write a Sentence: And How to Read One.*

Fogarty, Mignon. *The Grammar Devotional.*

Strunk, William, Jr. and E. B. White. *The Elements of Style.*

Truss, Lynne. *Eats, Shoots & Leaves: The Zero Tolerance Approach to Punctuation.*

On the Writing Life

Beach, Sylvia. *Shakespeare and Company.*

Calvino, Italo. *If on a winter's night a traveler.*

Chetkovich, Kathryn. "Envy," anthologized in *The Best American Essays 2004.*

Edmundson, Mark. *Why Read?*

Dillard, Annie. *The Writing Life.*

Goldberg, Natalie. *Writing Down the Bones: Freeing the Writer Within.*

Gladwell, Malcolm. "The Science of the Sleeper." www.gladwell.com.

Hemingway, Ernest. *A Moveable Feast.*

King, Steven. *On Writing: A Memoir of the Craft.*

Lamott, Anne. *Bird by Bird: Some Instructions on Writing and Life.*

Lerner, Betsy. *The Forest for the Trees: An Editor's Advice to Writers.*

One Hundred Famous Rejections. http://www.onehundred rejections.com.

Quindlen, Anna. *How Reading Changed My Life.*

SARK. *A Creative Companion: How to Free Your Creative Spirit.*

Woolf, Virginia. *A Room of One's Own.*

For Writing Exercises and Smart Thinking About How Writing Is Made

Baxter, Charles. *Burning Down the House: Essays on Fiction.*

Bell, Madison Smartt. *Narrative Design: A Writer's Guide to Structure.*

Benke, Karen. *Rip the Page!: Adventures in Creative Writing.*

Dunn, Jessica, and Danielle Dunn. *A Teen's Guide to Getting Published: Publishing for Profit, Recognition, and Academic Success.*

Gardner, John. *The Art of Fiction: Notes on Craft for Young Writers.*

Hanley, Victoria. *Seize the Story: A Handbook for Teens Who Like to Write.*

Kundera, Milan. *The Art of the Novel.*

Levine, Gail Carson. *Writing Magic: Creating Stories that Fly.*

Mazer, Anne, and Ellen Potter. *Spilling Ink: A Young Writer's Handbook.*

Thurston, Cheryl Miller. *Unjournaling.*

Zinsser, William. *On Writing Well: The Classic Guide to Writing Nonfiction.*

To Find Writing Classes, Programs, and Centers

- Figment offers online writing classes as well as opportunities to critique and be critiqued by a vast number of other writers. www.figment.com.

- Gotham Writers' Workshop started by offering writing workshops in New York City and went international when they went online. www.writingclasses.com.

- *Teen Ink* offers an excellent list of summer programs. www.teenink.com/Summer.

- 826 National started with a writing center founded in 2002 by Dave Eggers and Ninive Calegari, at 826 Valencia Street in San Francisco. Satellites have been popping up steadily ever since, all over the nation. They might already be near you, or be coming soon. www.826national.org.

- Writopia Lab offers workshops and summer camps in New York, Washington DC, and Los Angeles, and they do online Skype sessions for students all over the world. www.writopialab.org.

- If you're not near an 826 National, or Richard Hugo House (Seattle, Washington), or The Telling Room (Portland, Maine), Google "writing center" or "teen writing workshop" with your hometown in the search. There are lots of them across the country. Ask at your local bookstore and library, too.

To Find an Agent, Publisher, or Literary Journal

- Okay, I may be biased, but Writer's Digest offers some pretty excellent books on finding agents, publishers, and literary journals, in every genre, especially in their annual Guide To series (as in *2013 Guide to Literary Agents*). www.writersdigestshop.com.
- *Jeff Herman's Guide to Publishers, Editors, and Literary Agents* has been around forever, with regular updates, for a reason—it's a polished, one-stop resource for writers.
- A few months' subscription to the Publishers Marketplace website may be worth the investment when you're looking for an agent—it's a comprehensive guide to industry professionals and publishing news and deals. www.publishersmarketplace.com.
- When vetting agents, check out the Association of Authors' Representatives website (www.aaronline.org). Agents are required to uphold certain bylaws in order to join, so if you see an agent listed as a member of the AAR, you can be sure that they are on the up and up. (Some disreputable agents will charge a reading fee, for example, but AAR agents are prohibited from doing that.)
- Literary Market Place has a searchable website and print book that provides loads of information on book publishers and agents. www.literarymarketplace.com.

For Time Management

Morgenstern, Julie. *Time Management from the Inside Out: The Foolproof System for Taking Control of Your Schedule and Your Life*

Zerubavel, Eviatar. *The Clockwork Muse: A Practical Guide to Writing Theses, Dissertations, and Books.*